THE CONFESSIONS OF ANNABEL BROWN AGED 59¾

The Confessions of Annabel Brown Aged 59¾

ANN WARREN

KINGSWAY PUBLICATIONS
EASTBOURNE

ISBN 0 85476 847 5

Text illustrations supplied courtesy of the author.

Published by
KINGSWAY PUBLICATIONS
Lottbridge Drove, Eastbourne, BN23 6NT, England.
E-mail: books@kingsway.co.uk

Designed and produced for the publishers by
Bookprint Creative Services, P.O. Box 827, BN21 3YJ, England.
Printed in Great Britain.

Contents

1

Trying to Enthuse about Being 'Over the Hill'

Woke up with a start just as the dawn chorus was reaching its full volume crescendo. Much as I love those birds during the daytime, I do wish they'd keep the decibels down when I am still trying to sleep!

Lay in bed dozing and tried to avoid thinking about all the really 'useful' things I could be doing if I actually got out of bed.

And then it kept going over and over in my mind how impossible it seems that I have arrived at this time of life already. When I look in the mirror it almost feels as if there must be some mistake – rather like a kind of time warp. Inside of me there is this lively energetic being who is still theoretically young and active, but the only problem seems to be that my body doesn't quite agree with this perception. . . .

I can remember thinking when I was still in my twenties and thirties that 'old age' was still a million miles away and the whole of life stretched out before me. Getting old was something that happened to other people and not to me for goodness sake!

Was I overenthusiastic and impossibly optimistic at that stage of life I wonder? Somehow the sky seemed the limit then, and it felt as if there were no boundaries and no end to the possibilities. There was always that new goalpost to head for or that new possibility lying enticingly up ahead, but now it feels as if I have accidentally reached and driven past the summit of my life without ever realizing it – and suddenly everything up ahead looks ominously downhill.

> When as a child I slept and wept, time crept,
> When as a youth I laughed and talked, time walked,
> When I became a full grown man, time ran,
> And – older I daily grew, time flew,
> Soon I shall find travelling on, time gone.[1]

How does one enthuse about travelling down the far side of the hill I wonder? I suppose at least it is, or it should be, much less work because the slope just carries one along instead of having to pedal frantically. Maybe it's got something to do with learning just to 'be' rather than to 'do'. But somehow I don't think I was made for this . . . or maybe I have just lost the final page of the instruction booklet?

How on earth does one think positively about going to collect the pension from the Post Office, tottering towards the zimmer frame, and even the possibility of an old people's home?

But when I ask God about this I realize he has a very different perspective from mine. 'Where are you actually heading?' he asks me. 'And how much have you thought about that part of the journey? And as a matter of interest what are you packing to take with you – because you can't take all this with you when you go? What are you doing now that will be of real lasting value to you and make you ready for life in my kingdom?'

I suppose that is a large part of the problem. If I am honest, heaven is still not a very real place to me, and much of what I imagine doesn't appeal to me in the least! Unhelpful images of endless boring church services, heavy Victorian-style angels suspended in old master paintings, or crowds of very artificially religious people sort of linger in the mind!

Of course, I know that it won't be like that. Just those few simply wonderful moments that we catch here on earth when Jesus comes unexpectedly very close – perhaps an overwhelming sense of his love at the communion rail, the touch of a little trusting child, or the glimpse of a baby fox cub drinking deeply from the pond in our garden – those few precious seconds when heaven momentarily reaches down to earth make us long for the mere whisper of eternity to last for ever.

C S Lewis talks about a 'desire for our own far off country . . . the scent of a flower we have not found, the echo of a tune we have not heard, news from a country we have never yet visited'.[2] I really like the sound of that. Maybe if I adjusted my viewfinder to bring heaven more into focus it would actually help.

2

Monday Morning

Looked hard in the mirror this morning and really wished I hadn't. Admittedly it's a bright sunny day and in the clear light from our bedroom window all the worst wrinkles were showing up, but even so. . . . However young I still feel on the inside, this is what other people round me are looking at when they see me, and if I'm honest it's a pretty depressing picture.

Despite all this so-called anti-wrinkle cream, and enough vitamin tablets to make me rattle, the fact of the matter is that this is 'me' today now. And there's no running away from it.

It must be very tough for those who start out in life being really beautiful – though actually that's never been my problem! Those bleary shadows under the eyes and the crow's feet must be so disheartening if you once looked like Jean Symmonds or Marilyn Monroe.

Tried to think of all the people I know and like who are not particularly wonderful to look at, and then realized that it's a different quality I'm seeing in them – something that shines through from within and makes me disregard what my eyes are telling me.

I never stop to think what Elaine looks like, because I

know what makes up her personality and why she is so special to me, and I suppose that is what I am really seeing. They say that most men still see their wives as they always used to look – that's just as well! (I certainly hope George does.) Maybe those wrinkles don't show up quite so much after all!

Mary is the person who always springs to mind on days like this. She really is the most amazing character. Despite being almost totally paralysed by polio at nineteen she somehow always appears full of life and energy, unendingly fascinated by what is going on around her. It's hard to believe that she had to live in a respirator for months, and has spent two thirds of her life as a quadriplegic imprisoned in a wheelchair, and dependent on her companion for almost everything.

When I am talking to her I can almost feel her daring me to think of her as anything other than perfectly normal – and as a result that's exactly what I see! She always seems so involved with everything that is going on around that sometimes I almost expect to see her climb out of her wheelchair. She is so very alive. I often wonder what her secret is . . . I certainly hope that I can be like that if I am still around in twenty years' time!

Decided to ask God to help me forget about becoming gradually more ancient and wrinkly.

Thought for the day: try to remember that 'Man looks at the outward appearance, but the Lord looks at the heart' (1 Samuel 16:7). After all, I suppose that all the worry and laughter lines on our faces are rather like honourable battle scars that tell people what we are really like on the inside, as well as what we have been through.

'The human face cannot keep its secret life if the owner wears it long enough,' says Alexis Carrel. 'Youth is a disguise, concealing character and disposition, but with advancing years the truth comes out.' Goodness, that's quite an alarming thought!

Tried to think of some of the really exceptional old folk that I have known. Often all their warmth and character begin to shine out through their faces in later life, just like an outward sign of all the good things that had been growing in secret all those years.

I'm asking God to keep me really close to him so that I can give this love out to others around me, and not turn into one of those terrible crabby old people whose bitter character shows all too clearly on their faces. I certainly know that I can't do this on my own without his help!

Later

Agatha Christie is reported to have said that it was wonderful being married to an archaeologist because the older she got the more interested he became in her. A wise old friend once told me that the older we get the more clearly we can see. It's a bit like climbing the steps of a tower; the view gradually becomes clearer and more extensive.

As the evening twilight fades away,
The sky is filled with stars invisible by day.

Henry Wadsworth Longfellow

3

Surely I Can't Be Nearly Sixty Already?

23rd August

Woke up in the middle of the night panicking again about being at this frightening threshold on the brink of sixty.

Everyone is trying to encourage me to think about this stage of life positively. Someone even said I should hold a birthday party – what, with sixty candles groaning on the cake?

Just at the moment I really wouldn't mind slipping away unnoticed and growing old quietly in the shrubbery or somewhere out of sight.

George is keeping very quiet these days as well. I'm not sure if he just feels unsure about having a wife with a free bus pass, or if he is being quietly smug because he got there several years before me, but I think I'll wait for a good day before I ask him.

The young are all being patronizingly supportive. I'm sure if we lived in the States they'd be buying me a rocking chair for the porch, or giving me a subscription to a health farm or a regular blue rinse.

This morning Gilly arrived with a wonderful example of her first attempt at pottery and insisted on putting it in pride of place on the most visible shelf in the sitting room – a delightful ornamental platter with my name and date of birth blazoned in large white letters round the rim. Needless to say everyone who has been in the room since has asked me the same question: 'What's so special about that day then?'! I'm obviously going to have to think up some kind of convincing story, or just face the facts. . . .

Decided I had better ask God to give me a more positive view of approaching my free bus pass, as I obviously wasn't going to get very far on my own, and then I found these verses about ageing trees in the Psalms:

They will flourish in the courts of our God.
They will still bear fruit in old age,
They will stay fresh and green. . . (Psalm 92:13–14)

That reminds me so vividly of those two fantastic cedar trees in the cloisters at Salisbury Cathedral.

Flourishing in old age is quite a thought! Though personally at this moment in time no one in their right mind could describe me as 'flourishing' and it all sounds impossibly optimistic. It probably doesn't help that I spent yesterday cleaning out our very untidy storeroom and today every bone in my body seems to be reminding me of that fact.

Cedar trees are apparently renowned for their majestic appearance and for the fact that they are still full of sap when very old, which seems to me like a great thought for this time of life.

I have always loved these trees and especially their wonderful spreading branches that seem to reach out and shelter all those who come close to them. It makes me think of some of the amazing old people I have known with seemingly indomitable spirits who kept going right to the very end, taking a real interest in everyone around them. Could I ever be like that? I'm honestly not sure. . . .

4

The Body Is Creaking a Bit

Friday

When I creaked out of bed this morning I really wanted to reach for the oil can. Wouldn't it be wonderful if we had lubrication points to get the joints moving a bit more smoothly first thing in the morning? Maybe I should just mention this small design fault to the Almighty, but then again maybe he doesn't see things in quite the same way.

In my mind's eye I have already been for a long walk, done my exercises and am ready to do a whole host of other things – but some-  how the body doesn't seem quite so enthusiastic! Maybe I should just shut my mind to all this and just get moving anyway?

George said it was time for us to go for a 'good bracing walk' to shake away the cobwebs. Honestly, he's always so keen it's almost painful, and he never seems to have off days like I do.

Rachel admitted last week that she had never understood why her old aunt used to go on and on about her aches and pains, but now she was beginning to find out with a vengeance. It's extraordinary how many people that I had always thought of as really fit and healthy are suddenly beginning to sprout bandages or straps to keep on playing any very active sport now. It's almost becoming a recognized badge of seniority down at the gym.

And those extra healthy types who were really keen athletes in their youth seem to be the worst hit of all, so maybe there's something to be said for being a couch potato after all.

According to the physiotherapist things like gardening and lifting grandchildren provide her with a very good continuous source of income from our age bracket. Well I'm glad it makes someone feel better!

I suppose it's more difficult for some of us to learn to slow down than others. I just seem to have spent my whole life on the go, and 'taking things quietly' really doesn't come naturally. Perhaps I could begin to enjoy it? Take half the morning to read the paper, gaze out of the window for a while, write all those letters I have been meaning to write? I suppose anything is possible, but I suspect that some kind of sledgehammer might be required!

At times like this I always think of our old vicar who technically retired nearly twenty years ago. He is still tearing around putting the world to rights and organizing all kinds of people to do interesting things in the neighbourhood. Last year he even grazed his shins riding around on his equally ancient motorbike, which finally shook him up a bit. Eventually someone had to point out to him that at around eighty travelling on a motorbike was not entirely usual!

But it's quite a difficult question really – how do you know when it's time to take life a bit easier, to stop doing all the things you usually do? Or does it all stop of its own accord? Personally I never even thought about it until someone remarked the other day that if I didn't watch out I could still be doing all the same things I do now in twenty years' time . . . and it didn't sound such a good idea!

Still, I don't believe there is such a thing as real full-time retirement – somehow it feels like giving up. But I expect that eventually the body probably just goes on strike. Or that's certainly how mine feels at the moment. I can almost hear it saying 'No, I am not going to support you through another year like the last one. Just forget it – or you can rest assured that I will have something very unpleasant and achy to inflict on you. . . .'

I started asking God how to cope on the bad days, and then I remembered St Paul complaining about his thorn in the flesh and begging God three times to take this away. Instead he is told, 'My grace is sufficient for you, for my power is made perfect in weakness' (2 Corinthians 12:10).

I suppose I'm not very good at coping with any kind of physical weakness, and like to feel I can stay in control of my own life. Anyway, I have decided that from now on I'm going to make every effort to stay fit and healthy for as many years as possible.

'God only helps those who help themselves.' I can just hear Mrs Forsyte-Williams' determined high-pitched voice reciting these words as I write. . . .

5 a.m.

Woke up in a tangle of rumpled duvet with George snoring loudly into my left earhole and started thinking again about 'independence'.

Extraordinary how difficult I sometimes find it to learn to trust God with the task of planning out my life for me. After all I've seen so many times that I can really trust him with the future, especially when I remember to pray about things, but somehow this all seems to go right against my very independent spirit! Unfortunately I still want to do it 'my way'.

Thinks ... I wonder if that's the reason why Frank Sinatra's song 'I did it my way' has become such a favourite at funerals?

Have just rediscovered this wonderful old prayer written by a seventeenth-century nun:

Lord thou knowest better than I know myself that I am growing older and will some day be old. Keep me from the fatal habit of thinking I must say something on every subject and on every occasion. Release me from craving to straighten out everybody's affairs. Make me thoughtful but not moody, helpful but not bossy. With my vast store of wisdom it seems a pity not to use it all, but thou knowest Lord that I want a few friends at the end.

Keep my mind free from the recital of endless details; give me wings to get to the point. Seal my lips on my aches and pains. They are increasing and a love of rehearsing them is becoming sweeter as the years go by. I dare not ask for grace enough to enjoy the tales of other's pains, but help me to endure them with patience.

I dare not ask for improved memory, but for a growing humility and a lessening cocksureness when my memory seems to clash with the memories of others. Teach me the glorious lesson that occasionally I may be mistaken.

Keep me reasonably sweet; I do not want to be a saint – some of them are hard to live with – but a sour old person is one of the crowning works of the devil. Give me the ability to see good things in unexpected places and talents in unexpected people. And give me, O Lord, the grace to tell them so. Amen.[3]

5

Not Long Before George Retires — Help!

Just realized this morning that George is due to retire in a few months' time and started wondering again how on earth he is going to cope stuck inside these four walls with no other 'staff' to organize. I just hope he doesn't want to start on me instead!

Marjorie Ringold down at the Club insisted that her poor Fred should spend the daytime out in the garden room because she didn't want him under her feet the whole time. He always looks a bit pathetic, rather like a bloodhound with nowhere to go. I wonder what she feeds him?

All the same I am not sure I want George trailing round after me asking me why I am doing what I am doing from morning to night. I know his father used to drive poor ma-in-law nearly crazy when he had nothing else to do after being forcibly retired at some ripe old age. Help! Just watch this space. . . .

I also have a sneaking suspicion that George is expecting me to fit neatly into the yawning gap that will be left by his super-efficient secretary Joyce, and I can just hear his voice now telling me to 'Take a letter' or some such! Shall have to keep dropping forceful-sounding hints about how busy I am, and how I have my own plans and need to keep a bit of space for myself. . . .

It's difficult really as I want him to look forward to retiring and to being at home, but on the other hand I definitely don't want some kind of takeover bid. Have heard a lot from older friends about how swamped they feel and have just realized that I will really have to start praying about how best to play this.

Help! Have just remembered that when Mabel's husband retired, he announced that he expected a cooked meal at lunchtime just as he'd always had at work – and she actually fell in with this!

If George wants a cooked meal then he is going to have to learn to cook it! And that's another thing – I honestly don't think he even knows how to boil an egg. Anyway, as a friend of mine said whilst on this subject, 'I married my husband for life and not for lunch.'

Jean's husband has been going to 'Man in the Kitchen' at their local Adult Education place and actually cooks her at least one meal a week – brilliant! Shall have to keep dropping hints, although I already know he is not at all keen.

Think I really need to talk to one or two of my older friends to see how they coped with all this. I expect he is every bit as worried about his retirement as I am! It must be very difficult for a man to suddenly have to give up all his responsibilities and just become an ordinary citizen again. And like most men he really only seems to have friends amongst the people he works with.

Do not be anxious about anything, but in everything, by prayer and petition, with thanksgiving, present your requests to God. And the peace of God, which transcends all understanding, will guard your hearts and your minds in Christ Jesus. (Philippians 4:6–7)

That's all very well, but 'worrying' seems to come very naturally indeed and I can conjure all kinds of terrible scenarios that never actually happen on the day. 'Why pray when you can worry?' as a wise old friend of mine always used to teasingly say.

5 a.m. again

Oh dear . . . thinking about the whole dreaded retirement scenario. I wonder if the trouble lies with our whole image of this? Whenever the word 'retire' is used in English it seems to have very negative depressing overtones: 'retiring' because of defeat in battle, or 'retiring exhausted' from the race, or in other words, on the way out!

But apparently the French have a saying 'Recouler pour mieux sauter' which means withdrawing in order to advance successfully.

'This', says John Eddison, 'should be the Christian way of regarding old age, and immediately invests retirement with a new significance and a new importance in preparing us for the after life – not an isolated period of slow and steady decay – but a time of mental, emotional and spiritual growth – an overture rather than a finale.'[4]

Time out of the rush of life to prepare for a whole new world ahead? That way we are not talking about travelling downhill, but instead going on up in a straight line with a definite purpose in mind. I think I could live with that idea. . . .

6

What Do They Mean, 'Too Old' at Sixty?

Tuesday 13th September

Heard this morning that Jane has just been told she can't go on running the Thrift Shop because at sixty she has 'suddenly become' too old. Apparently she wasn't too old a month ago, but she is now. Honestly, you do wonder. . . .

This whole wonderful project to help the unemployed was entirely her idea in the first place – she set it up, she found the people to help get the thing off the ground – and it is her sunny good nature and kindness that has kept it running so successfully all these years. What do they mean 'too old'?

I simply can't imagine how it will run without her, and neither can I think of a single person who will put in the necessary energy or time. But apparently 'the book says' that at sixty she is no longer fit to do this, so that's the end of the matter. A younger person will 'of course' do the job much better.

I know the same kind of thing has happened to several other people around the parish, but it has never come so close to home before. Needless to say poor Jane feels as if she has just been put out on the scrap heap, but is too embarrassed to tell people what has happened or why.

What on earth do they think they are doing? If I come

across the chairman I certainly feel like giving him a piece of my mind. But George says I mustn't interfere or it will only make things worse. What does he think I'll do? Certainly there are quite a few interesting possibilities. . . .

It's really started me thinking about this whole automatic retirement deadline and why it has to be assumed that at a certain age – regardless of success or ability – one is automatically assumed to be 'over the hill', 'past it' or no longer able to 'keep up to speed'.

Sometimes it's obviously necessary. I doubt if John was still really getting through the work as well as he used to when they asked him to retire – and he seemed quite relieved once he had got over the shock. And though George will miss his job, he is really looking forward to a break from all the pressure and time to enjoy life a bit more. Anyway it was always agreed that he would retire at this point in time.

But when you think about it, what exactly is supposed to happen at sixty that makes this age such an impossible hurdle? And why is it automatically assumed that any younger person can do the same job so much better? I know I sound like a defender of 'grey power' but honestly this is just the kind of experience that can make you question the whole system.

Have the same feeling even in church sometimes. They sort of tolerate us doing things, but would much rather we were ten or fifteen years younger.

Now of course there are a great many other things that I would be more than happy to be told I was too old to do – like digging the garden, or ironing George's shirts, or the spring cleaning – but no one seems too worried about all that. I wonder why? Just think how wonderful it would be to be pensioned off from all these chores!

7

About to Become a Grandmother

Only another few weeks till I become a grandmother –
simultaneously an amazing and a terrifying thought!
'Will it feel any different?' I wonder.

Come to that I find it almost impossible to imagine
Carol as a mother! It doesn't seem all that long ago that I
was changing her nappies. I just hope she will cope all
right – she seems so scatty sometimes. No doubt I am
worrying unnecessarily as usual, but I simply hate the
thought of her having to go through labour and all that.
I'm really sad that they are moving up north at just this
time. But at least it will stop me being a doting and ever-
present grandmother (though let's face it that's extremely unlikely as I was never a particularly doting mother!).
And one big plus is that it means I can't possibly
become a permanently available babysitter! But still, I'm
really going to miss them terribly.

They heard yesterday that the house won't be ready
to move into until just a week before the baby is due –
impossible! I can just imagine Carol having to unpack
cases and move furniture around with that enormous
bump right in the way. It worries me and I really wish
she would take things a bit easier. But amazingly neither

of them seems remotely phased by all of this upheaval.

I don't think they have the least idea of what is about to hit them. Absolutely nothing seems to be ready for this poor little mite, but they keep telling me not to worry as they can 'get everything up in Scotland' when they arrive. . . .

Somehow I think this baby seems just like another puppy to them. I must say I really would like to be somewhere closer just in case we're needed, but Carol tells me I am fussing – and she's probably right.

Why is it so difficult to just walk away and let one's young live their own lives and make their own mistakes?

If I'm honest I still remember my parents offering me 'helpful' advice and just wishing they would shut up! It's amazing how different everything feels when you are offering your own 'pearls of wisdom' and no one wants to know. But no doubt we all seem just as 'fuddy duddy' and out of touch as our parents used to.

Today's good resolution: Remember what a pain it was to be at the receiving end of unwanted parental 'advice'.

Of course it would all be very different if we lived in India, or somewhere in the Far East, where the young would hang on our every word and accord us with 'the respect we deserve'. Now there's a thought!

George made an interesting observation this morning: Our trouble is that we were always expected to do exactly what our parents wanted, no questions asked, and these days we are always being told we should fit in with the children and recognize that we've 'had our day'. The only thing is he can't quite remember exactly when our day was.

It sounds a bit cynical but I suspect he has got a point. Anyway at least we have managed to arrange to be in

Scotland on holiday at around the time this baby is due, which certainly makes me feel better. If we're not actually staying with them (where it's bound to be chaos anyway!), then we can be around to do our grandparent appreciation bit when this new little creature arrives, and can also pick up the pieces with any removal crisis if necessary.

Goodness I have found a verse in Ecclesiastes that actually tells us 'Do not say, "Why were the old days better than these?" For it is not wise to ask such questions' (Ecclesiastes 7:10). It's quite a thought that exactly the same things were happening all those years ago — pleased to know I got it right as well.

Today's other timely thought is also from Ecclesiastes. **NB!** 'There is a time to be silent and a time to speak.'

I have found that the best way to give advice to children is to find out what they want and then advise them to do it.

Harry Truman

When I was a boy of fourteen my father was so ignorant I could hardly stand to have the old man around. But when I got to be twenty-one, I was astonished at how much he had learnt in seven years.

Mark Twain

8

That Dreaded Retirement Seminar

Really dreading this wretched seminar tomorrow. Why does George land me with these kinds of things?

He seems to have had so many sessions on 'Retirement' provided by the company. 'How to Look After Your Finances' – he was fairly morose for at least a week after that one! 'Trying Your Hand at DIY' – which of course brought on that perfectly hideous effort at carpentry still hidden away in the shed. And honestly I've lost track of how many others. I'm sure it's a very good thing – but not at all sure why he needs to involve me in 'Understanding Your Personality'. In fact just thinking about this makes me feel quite uncomfortable.

George was talking about this with John and Caroline when we met up with them last month, and it almost felt as if they were trying to put me into some neat little box and tell me how I ought to be behaving. Not my scene at all, thank you very much.

All I have been told is that it has something to do with relating to all sorts of different personalities and what this means in the light of retirement and spending a lot of time together . . . and then a whole string of incomprehensible letters just guaranteed to make me feel uneasy.

I suppose I'll have to go just to keep George happy –
but I intend to keep my own counsel and tell nobody
anything. Honestly, what a waste of time!

Friday evening

What fun and what an absolutely wonderful day – a real
shaft of sunlight through what looked like being a
dreadfully boring seminar. So many things explained at
one hit, and so great to be given permission to be
myself, and not take any notice when other people tell
me I should be 'more organized', or 'more persevering',
or 'more detached' or whatever the current complaint is.
Myers Briggs sounded such a terrible mouthful of a
name, and by the time I had finished filling in all those
dreadful questions about how I react in different situa-
tions, I really just wanted to throw the whole thing in
the bin.

But now suddenly, perhaps for the first time in my life,
I am beginning to realize that we are all different, because
we were made that way, and because we need all these
different abilities and gifts around in the world. At long
last I can accept that 'it's okay to be me' and I don't have
to feel guilty because I am not like Jane or George.

Now I know I was *meant to be* some kind of enthusiastic ideas person, and not some amazingly efficient organizer or businesswoman. That my personality type naturally loves things like art and music – and that doesn't
make me 'impossibly arty' as George usually implies;
that I do get bored easily, and I am *not* particularly good
at finishing things off, unless someone gives me a deadline. And yes, everything is often done in one almighty
last minute rush – but at least it does get done, although
George never believes me when I tell him it will!

30

Above all I suppose that the most helpful thing I found was quite simply the permission to 'be myself' and not to feel that I have to be like George, or anyone else for that matter. What a wonderful relief!

Think George might feel that I have been somehow let off the hook, and that I ought to be more 'systematic' and 'tidy minded' just like he is. Shall have to keep remembering that as a 'J' he is a natural organizer.

And of course I know now why he feels he has to try and organize me and to put what he sees as the chaos of my world to rights. Obviously I am going to have to find him something else to organize, just to take his mind off me and my way of doing things!

Feel so guilty now about how I have always misunderstood 'thinking' people and wrongly assumed that they didn't care about others. It's really helpful to understand that they show their love and care in completely different and very practical ways.

I had never really understood before that when George did something practical for me – like filling up the car with petrol or doing the washing up – this was his way of showing his love for me. Instead I've spent my whole life wishing he would use lots of caring emotional words, without ever realizing that this kind of 'gushing' (as he would call it!) could never come naturally to him in a million years.

Why on earth didn't anyone tell me this before? It would certainly have saved me a great deal of heartache.

But now we know we are so very different – and of course opposites attract – so this just underlines the need to find different outlets in retirement, different things to do, and the right things to do together.

Wonderful news! George has just told me that he is planning a special trip 'down under' for my sixtieth birthday – can hardly believe it! We shall be able to visit all our old friends and get some real winter sunshine. That's *so* kind of him. Suddenly feeling really excited about my birthday after all.

9

Gruesome Twosomes

Yesterday's seminar really got me thinking about Tony and Shirley. They seem so utterly miserable since he retired. She was perfectly happy in her own little world with her own friends and doing the things that were important to her, but now that he is there all the time, seeming to want to control her, she seems to have almost given up (suppose he must be an organizing 'J' like George).

The poor man probably feels rather like being a sheepdog with no sheep to round up!

He doesn't even like her seeing her closest friends any more, as if he is almost jealous of any time she spends without him. Really it's ridiculous, when you think of all those years that he expected her to cope whilst he was running the office.

But at the same time I reckon it's really up to her to come out and say what she is feeling and just make some space for herself. The trouble is she has always been rather timid, and I suspect she just can't cope with the strength of his personality. I can see now that she is probably a 'feeling' kind of person and doesn't want to upset him – but she is going to have to tell him how she feels because he clearly doesn't know.

But it does all make you realize why retirement is such a major adjustment, and why some of us need all the help we can get to understand what is going on and make the necessary changes.

It sometimes feels as if she has given up on her own life altogether and allowed Tony to take over completely – but you can see that neither of them is really happy as a result of this. She feels she can't breathe without his permission, and he feels completely trapped in her world, obviously missing the breadth and interest of all his work at the bank. Maybe they should do this course so that they can find their way out of this particular jungle?

There's something about 'gruesome twosomes' that always seems to give this paralysing clinging impression of mutual self-interest – as if people are desperately trying to find happiness by almost devouring one another, rather like two stems of convolvulus that have been frantically winding round and round each other, whilst neither one has the inner strength to hold the other up.

I reckon that common sense should tell us that in retirement of all times – when if we don't watch out we could be stuck indefinitely within the same four walls together! Then we are going to badly need a few different interests to pursue, so that at the very least we will have something to talk about when we are alone.

The Johnstones down the road seem to spend their whole lives helping other people and getting involved in every possible activity that needs them, together or separately, and as a result they are never bored or friendless and obviously very happy together. Though they probably never have the time even to think about whether they are or not!

What was it Jesus said about this? 'For whoever wants to save his life will lose it, but whoever loses his life for me will save it' (Luke 9:24).

10

Scotland for Timothy's Birth

Thank goodness we decided to come up to Scotland early!

Arrived here on Saturday evening with just enough time to briefly inspect their tiny little house, climbing over all the chaos and the remains of the packing cases, before heading off down the road to fall into bed in the nearest B & B.

Carol said they wanted to be left in peace on Sunday after church to get everything sorted out in their own way, and so we tactfully left them to it and withdrew to take ourselves for a walk up the Glen. Honestly I think we must be getting wiser in our old age! I didn't once hear myself say in my usual tactless way *anything* about what a tip the place still was or suggest that I could help organize things for them. Amazing!

Rang Tony as soon as we got home from our walk, just to check that all was well and that Carol was all ready for our mammoth 'baby shopping' expedition the following morning, and found that the poor man had been frantically trying to contact us all afternoon. Our first grandson had already arrived, nearly a week earlier than expected, and Carol was just longing for us to get over to the hospital and see him.

Rushed down to Perth Royal Infirmary just in time for the last hour of visiting time, clutching the only vaguely suitable thing we could find in the local shop – a bunch of rather limp and not very inspiring white spider chrysanthemums.

Carol was propped up in bed looking rosy and triumphant, and it was very difficult to take in the fact that this tiny little creature in her arms was actually our grandson and a new start for the family of the next generation. He seemed so fragile he could easily break at any minute. How quickly one forgets that all of ours were this small once – or for that matter what to do with a new baby! I imagine we'll be on one very steep relearning curve from now on, starting with disposable nappies – a really major blessing!

The hospital seemed understandably bemused by the fact that they had absolutely nothing for the baby to wear, and so inevitably the famous shopping expedition that Carol and I had planned for Monday landed fairly and squarely onto the shoulders of two extremely green and inexperienced grandparents. . . .

I will never forget the raised eyebrows of shop assistants as we set out to buy this mammoth list of baby gear down in Edinburgh. You could well imagine the thought bubbles emerging from their heads: 'What on earth are these wrinklies doing looking for all this baby gear? Surely they aren't planning some weird last minute venture of their own?'

Finally in desperation – since we really didn't even recognize half the things they were asking for – we managed to find ourselves a wonderful homely Scots lassie, who looked as if she was more than used to looking after a family of at least six, and perfectly capable of coping with two lost looking grandparents.

'Och yes – you'll be needing several pairs of those,' she intoned, in that wonderful accent that I could listen to for hours. 'Well I find this kind of carrycot just fine, and will you no be needing the frame that goes with it as well?'

So in the end, entirely and only thanks to this wee lassie (or I think we would be there still), we actually completed that mammoth list.

And then all the way back I was worrying about what would happen if they didn't like the colours and designs that we had bought.

But to our amazement both Tony and Carol seemed perfectly happy with everything, which I reckon was something of a minor miracle in itself! By this time I expect they were only too thankful to have anything at all for the baby to wear, but it was quite a relief just the same.

So now we get down to being new grandparents and tune in once again to the fascination of childhood and beginning the life cycle all over again. Extraordinary to think that all of us started out in life this tiny in the beginning. I tried to imagine some of the people we know as babies – which proved to be quite an intriguing exercise!

Probably the vicar looked much the same as he does now – round, rosy and cherubic, with very little hair. But Mr Ponsonby on the other hand – the mind boggles! I really wonder what he looked like before acquiring those terrifying eyebrows and angry looking expression. He might even have looked quite sweet, or any sensible woman would probably have abandoned him at birth!

What a truly wonderful thing the gift of life is, and how easily we forget this.

Our birth is but a sleep and a forgetting:
The Soul that rises with us, our life's Star,
Hath had elsewhere its setting,
And cometh from afar:
Not in entire forgetfulness,
And not in utter nakedness,
But trailing clouds of glory do we come
From God, who is our home:
Heaven lies about us in our infancy!

William Wordsworth[5]

Praying that we can catch a fresh glimpse of this child-hood joy, and that we can help this little mite keep his sense of wonder and awe and one day discover a real faith for himself.

11

Sixty-Year-Olds Have Never Had It So Good?

12th November

Have just found an article in the paper this morning guaranteed to fill all of us wrinklies with hope and telling us that people 'of our age' have never had it so good – holidays, vitamins, exercise, and time to do whatever they want.

Our bathroom cabinets are loaded with Vitamins and Chinese medicines. Vitamin C and E to fight those nasty free radicals that helped carry off our fathers with cancer or heart disease; calcium to keep our bones strong and free from the dowager's hump that disfigured our grandmothers. Gingko biloba to ward off the absent mindedness that used to regularly land respectable middle aged women in dock for forgetting to pay for a packet of biscuits in the supermarket. Cod liver oil, zinc, dong quai so that we practically rattle when we walk, and of course we walk because we know that exercise is another anti ageing ploy.[6]

Well, if this is to be believed it sounds as if many of us could expect at least another twenty years of fit healthy living ahead of us – God willing – before we even begin to reach our dotage. Not sure what I feel about that but still. . . .

If my brother-in-law at eighty is anything to go by, then active life could go on a lot longer still. But then Henry has got to be the exception. He is so incredibly fit and energetic from living in the depths of the country and insisting on cycling everywhere, that both of us often feel absolutely exhausted after only a few hours with him . . . despite the fact that to him we are 'mere whippersnappers'.

I was listening to a large enthusiastic woman talking about her Bowls Club in the Post Office yesterday and telling everyone with enormous pride how madly keen they all are. It sounded quite a frightening prospect and a bit too hearty for me I'm afraid, but there was no question about her very real enjoyment of this.

Looking around, so many of our friends seem to have recently taken up croquet or golf, not to mention all those aerobics classes down at the gym every Wednesday, so there's no doubt that 'fitness' is all the rage, as George keeps telling me. Well I do still play tennis – after a fashion.

But I have to confess that all this frantic activity can seem a bit pointless to me sometimes – unless there is some real underlying purpose to people's lives. It sometimes sounds to me rather like oiling the machinery well just in order to keep it going, without first asking the really important questions about what the machine was intended to do in the first place. But then no doubt George would say I was being cynical again.

I read somewhere recently that more people die from lack of fulfilment than any other cause.

I suppose that's what is in the back of my mind really. Surely there can't be much genuine satisfaction in the kind of aimless lives that so many people seem to be living – with or without exercise – and no real sense of fulfilment when life itself seems rather meaningless and in effect nothing more than a way of filling up the time pleasantly? Or is this just me?

George says I can always be relied on to ask the really difficult questions that no one ever wants to hear.

Anyway what I need for our retirement – besides a bit of time to relax – is some wonderful new challenge to put a bit of dynamite under me. At the moment I'm not sure what this is going to be, but *I am sure* that God won't leave this empty space vacant for very long!

I read recently that 64 per cent of the greatest achievements of mankind have actually been undertaken by people in the last quarter of their lives, so that should galvanize us into some kind of activity!

The person who retires in good health and with ample reserves of energy and vigour will want something more than unlimited gardening or golf. He will want to do something which makes use of the gifts he has exercised for so long in his job, and with which he can continue to make a useful contribution to society.

It is often at this stage of life that a man or woman will be at their most useful and with plenty of mileage ahead. There is an almost unlimited number of charitable organizations, church societies, local clubs and institutions which would collapse or be seriously damaged if it were not for the continual stream of voluntary helpers from the ranks of the retired.

John Eddison[7]

Just looking round some of our friends to see what those we really respect are doing with their time.

One friend of ours takes blind people bowling and riding, several others have trained for the Citizen's Advice Bureau or prison visiting, one or two are visiting lonely old people in the area, and one is manning a counselling line for young people with problems.

But I honestly think 'the gold star' award has to go to our friend Janet who, despite being widowed barely two years ago, has been totally transformed since she visited the employment agency asking about voluntary work and what was really needed in the community.

It seems to me her feet have scarcely touched the ground since, and she is so obviously very much happier and more fulfilled in her life that it's truly wonderful to see!

Ask and it will be given to you; seek and you will find; knock and the door will be opened to you. For everyone who asks receives; he who seeks finds; and to him who knocks, the door will be opened. (Matthew 7:7–8)

Friday evening

Had a great time clearing out the dead wood from a whole lot of overgrown shrubs in the garden today – really satisfying stuff and totally exhausting. But looking at that corner now I can hardly believe the difference it has made.

And there tucked away under all that dead wood were a whole lot of fresh new shoots just waiting to be given a chance at life. If I hadn't taken all the dead

43

wood away I would never even have seen this, let alone given it a chance to live and grow when spring comes. Just hope that's a parable about what is to come.

Have come across quite a few people who really hated having to retire or being made redundant, but who as a result found a completely new direction in life that has really excited them – and which they would never have found any other way.

What is it people say? 'God never shuts a door unless he opens a window.'

12

Shock of Jeremy Dying in the Night

Terrible shock this morning to hear about Jeremy dying in the night. Can hardly believe it's happened – after all he was so young and only retired a few months ago. The whole parish is going round in a sort of mesmerized state of shock. We'll all miss him terribly and his cheerful enthusiastic presence around the place. Can't quite believe I won't see his untidy white mop of hair disappearing down the road with the dog tomorrow as usual or out there hacking away at the nettles by his gate.

He was one of those people who just seemed indestructible. I feel so sorry for his Eileen. Simply can't imagine how she will cope. They were such a devoted couple and she was so looking forward to his retirement.

I think what has shaken some of us most is the fact that he was only just sixty, and there is an unspoken thought around that this means it could have happened to any one of us. The silent question hanging in the air is 'Could I be next?'

Actually I think it's already having quite a healthy sobering sort of effect on all of us. Suddenly people have started asking why they are keeping on doing the same old things, when honestly they know deep down it is time to stop. Some folk are wondering what they are really saving up for, and thinking about what they would really want to do before time is up and it's too late – or before they get too old and creaky.

I suppose none of us knows what life has in store for us – and perhaps it's just as well! But there are an awful lot of people on some kind of treadmill who can't seem to stop and ask what they are doing or why.

I heard this very salutary thought recently: 'No man ever said on his death bed "I wish I'd spent more time at the office." '[8] It really made me think. . . .

Made a new resolution today – I am going to stop rushing around and ask myself regularly, 'If I knew that this was my last week on earth, how would I be spending the time?'

I often think it's so sad when people never get round to telling their children and their families and friends how much they love them.

It makes me think of Jane, whose parents died when she was very young, leaving her very few memories of them. She told me once how she would just love to have had something written down from them telling her that they really loved her, and a little about their hopes and prayers for her. I know it would have meant so much to her to know what they were feeling.

Had this wonderful idea of writing a special letter to each of the children telling them how much I love them and what my hopes and dreams for them are. But then I started worrying that they might find these before the due time and think I was off my rocker.

NB Have decided that I am going to do this anyway – after all none of us knows what tomorrow might bring . . . and I really want them to know how much they mean to me and how precious they all are.

The British are really hopeless at this kind of thing, but it matters so much when the opportunity for saying anything has gone for ever. So many people say that when a friend dies suddenly they regret words that were left unspoken and thoughtless actions unforgiven.

Have just realized that this is probably how Jesus was thinking just before his death, when he talked to his disciples in the Garden of Gethsemane about the future and how very much he loved and cared for each one of them:

Do not let your hearts be troubled. Trust in God; trust also in me. In my Father's house are many rooms; if it were not so, I would have told you. I am going there to prepare a place for you. And if I go and prepare a place for you, I will come back and take you to be with me that you also may be where I am. You know the way to the place where I am going. (John 14: 1–4)

When I'm Alone

I thought of age and loneliness and change,
I thought how strange we grow when we're alone,
And how unlike the selves that meet and talk,
And blow the candles out and say Goodnight
Alone. The word is life endured and known
It is the stillness where our spirits walk
And all but inmost faith is overthrown.

Siegfried Sassoon[9]

13

On Being Left Alone

Finally plucked up the courage to go and visit Eileen this morning, and I'm really glad I went. Poor love – it all happened so suddenly, and apparently no one realized that his heart was in such a dicky state. A terrible shock happening out of the blue like that – but I suppose it was a nice way for him to go.

All she wanted to do was to talk and talk about him and to have a really good cry, but already she senses that people are staying away because they don't know what to say. Yesterday she actually saw someone cross the street rather than have to talk to her. It makes me so angry when people do this! I know some folk don't know what to say and feel they ought to have some kind of helpful advice to give, but quite frankly that's the last thing anyone needs at such a time!

All you can really do I reckon is just 'be there' and listen ... there just aren't any easy answers to the whys and wherefores of life and death, and an awful lot of things I shall want answers to myself one day.

I suppose very occasionally, much later on in life we can begin to see a reason for things that have happened, but at this moment in time glib 'easy answers' and pious phrases can be a real turn off. Just hope Edith with some of the 'textbook' Bible verses she always trots out at this sort of time will keep well away from her. I think all we need to know is that God is deeply concerned and feeling our pain with us. But honestly some people make me so angry! I suppose it's just embarrassment and people don't know what to say, but even so.

Poor Eileen – almost the worst thing about Jeremy's death is that it's so close to Christmas now and to all the plans they had to spend it with their children and grandchildren. I know that they will all look after her, but it's almost as if Christmas will be blackened for ever with this tragic memory – and something that she will find it so hard to escape from in the future.

14
Christmas with the Family

Christmas at last and all that dreadful pressure of 'so many shopping days to go' has finally departed from our television screens, so that we can actually settle down to remembering what it's all about and to enjoying this very special day together.

When I'm doing this frantic shop for all the family and their presents, I sometimes get this quite sick feeling in the pit of my stomach, and just long to take a bit of time to listen to what God is saying about it all. I'm sure he never meant his birthday to be celebrated like this!

Just thinking of how lovely it was when we lived abroad and there was no commercial pressure of any kind. They only remembered to put up the rather tatty Christmas lights along the main street just a couple of days beforehand, and you were very lucky even to be able to buy a turkey or any other Western goodies.

But it was lovely just to take time out to sing carols by candlelight down by the sea, with nothing but the sound of the waves to disturb the peace, and the brilliant archway of Pacific stars simply filling the sky overhead. No problem imagining choirs of angels in that setting!

That's what I love about the midnight service – it's

just so special to come back out into the cold night air and look up into the December sky and realize that this is The Day when he entered our world and when it all started.

It's great to have some of the family back under the same roof again, though I suppose it will always seem a bit strange that one or other of them is usually missing and spending time with their in-laws. Really sad not to have Carol and Tony here and especially little Timothy. But I made up my mind ages ago never to have a fight about who spent Christmas with whom. It's amazing how many people do this, and then just end up ruining the day for everyone else.

Mark and Jenny seem to be in the middle of some pointless argument about the right way to spend Christmas day. She of course is convinced that what we do here is right, whilst his family pattern is completely different and 'right' to him. It's surprising what you can disagree about given half a chance, and Jenny has always had very strong views at the best of times!

Had better get to bed, or I will never manage to see tomorrow out. . . .

15

How about a Bit of Peace in Church?

Oh no, it's Sunday and we're back to jolly Family Service time again now that Christmas is over. It's just one of those mornings when I would love nothing better than a little bit of peace and quiet in church instead of all those enthusiastic choruses and children's activities.

Okay, so that sounds ancient and out of touch. But the way I feel today I could almost join the 'Bring back the Prayer Book Brigade' – travelling fast backwards to 1662, and losing myself safely in all that beautiful ringing emotive language of the past. It's amazing how when I was twenty years younger I simply couldn't understand why older people felt like this, but if I'm honest there are times when it is becoming crystal clear!

And while we're on the subject, does anyone happen to know why we have to sing all these choruses over and over and over again? Do we really believe that the Almighty is getting a bit deaf and didn't actually hear what we sang the first time round? Or are we trying to achieve more Brownie points by singing these not particularly brilliant words over and over again – you know, ten stars in heaven for surviving to rendering number three? By which time my legs are killing me, but I am usually too ashamed to admit defeat and sit down.

And whilst I am having a good old moan, perhaps we could ask why the entire Family Service seems to be geared to the mental age of five-year-olds? Haven't they noticed that there are a few older folk scattered around the congregation as well – even ten-year-olds and teenagers, let alone mums and dads and all of us wrinklies? It would be really nice sometimes to hear words of more than two syllables!

But then I keep telling myself how pleased the Almighty must be to see and hear all these noisy enthusiastic children – even though just at this moment I am definitely not! Maybe it will be different when I have older grandchildren and anything which keeps them happy and occupied will be fine by me . . . but not today I'm afraid.

Re-reading this I am not sure that I am even feeling in the right mood for church at all this morning.

George says we have to go because he is on sidesmen's duty – typical!

Later

Actually if I am honest it really wasn't that bad after all. The speaker was really genuine and down to earth, and a lot of what he said made complete sense to me.

And then afterwards I talked to dear old Barbara and saw her wonderful crinkly face burst into smiles as she watched all the children streaming out into the winter sunlight. It was so obvious that she really loves and cares about them even though she never had any children of her own – she puts me to shame sometimes. When the children were small she even used to thank us for asking her to babysit!

53

I suppose the apostles felt rather like I did this morning when they tried to keep the children away from Jesus to give him some peace:

When Jesus saw this, he was indignant. He said to them, 'Let the little children come to me, and do not hinder them, for the kingdom of God belongs to such as these. I tell you the truth, anyone who will not receive the kingdom of God like a little child will never enter it.' And he took the children in his arms, put his hands on them and blessed them. (Mark 10:14–16)

I stand corrected!

16

Made the Mistake of Weighing Myself

Made the terrible mistake of weighing myself this morning and really wished I hadn't.

It seems almost impossible to believe that I have gone up *one whole size* in clothes during the last few months. Even allowing for Christmas parties and too much time indoors close to the fridge, I really thought this was a bit extreme.

Anyway, in a moment of madness, and despite the unmistakeable evidence of so many clothes that failed to stretch round my middle any more, I made the stupid mistake of turning to the scales for some kind of contradiction. Needless to say this only made matters a great deal worse than they were before.

Honestly there was a time when I could eat absolutely anything and never put on so much as an ounce of weight – which some of my friends found pretty annoying. But now I know exactly how they felt.

How on earth does one change the habits of a lifetime?

George has been complaining for some time about his waistline – and it's true he is getting fairly (but quite pleasantly) rotund. He of course would 'call a spade a spade' and use the word 'fat'. But when I suggested we go on this diet someone gave us, the sudden enthusiasm for dieting disappeared rather rapidly.

And I have to admit that endless cold meat, tuna fish and beetroot are not my favourite foods either. I also found myself getting ravenously hungry between lunch and supper. But the great advantage of this particular diet was that after three days of it you could just go back and eat normally for the rest of the week.

According to them the theory is that you will lose eight to ten pounds each week doing this, but after just three days of hunger and horrible food I am not at all sure that it is worth it. 'No discipline', as George would say – but then I haven't exactly noticed him being that enthusiastic about it either.

Of course we could always go down to the gym or have another go at that fearsome series of exercises he is so fond of, but even thinking about this wears me out.

Something has got to happen though, or I am going to end up like one of those positively enormous ladies who have clearly given up completely and are just carrying on eating regardless in an effort to make themselves feel better.

But please God don't let me become that impossibly huge . . . I know it shouldn't matter that much, but I'm afraid it just does!

It's funny how you never believe what older people tell you. I can so well remember a rather large 'comfortable' friend in India telling me how slim and skeletal she used to be when she was younger, and taking this with a very large pinch of salt. And I guess not many people would believe me if I said that now!

Oh dear, am I never going to be able to sleep through the whole night ever again? Apart from anything else this time of day is so *boring*.

Found myself thinking about exercise and vitamins and health foods and wondering how much all this really matters in the scale of things – and just remembering the words of Jesus on this very subject:

> Do not worry about your life, what you will eat or drink; or about your body, what you will wear. Is not life more important than food, and the body more important than clothes? Look at the birds of the air; they do not sow or reap or store away in barns, and yet your heavenly Father feeds them. Are you not much more valuable than they? Who of you by worrying can add a single hour to his life? (Matthew 6:25–27)

NB Try to remember this when the flab is on the increase and nothing seems to fit any more – there are definitely more important things in life!

17
D Day

Well today is the day, so I had better gather up my courage in both hands and saunter downstairs looking as if nothing has happened, waiting for the young to pounce with enthusiastic birthday greetings – that is of course if they are actually out of bed. Or maybe I could escape out to the conservatory with a quiet cup of coffee, where with any luck it will take them some time to find me!

I would give anything just to be able to press a button and escape this particular hurdle, but it is clearly not going to be allowed. . . .

Whose birthday is this anyway? Personally I don't want to remember how old I am, and nor do I want any special presents in memory of an event that I would much rather forget – and I definitely don't want any big celebrations!

At least that's one of my achievements for today – refusing point blank to allow them to hold a 'special birthday party' in my honour. I know none of them really understands and it's very difficult to explain – but that's just too bad!

I wonder what used to happen in the last century?

Was this ripe old age a universal signal for ladies to withdraw to their chaises longues and demand the smelling salts if anything at all upset them or sounded like too much effort?

Come to that, it's not a bad idea – enough of all this keeping fit I say!

Perhaps we should all cash in and make the most of finally achieving this mammoth milestone? How about becoming a real tyrant in the manner of Lady Bracknell in *The Importance of Being Earnest*? I think I could even begin to enjoy that. The only trouble is that then there would be no one to cook or clean – and I am fairly sure that George wouldn't take to the idea at all! I strongly suspect he has that particular role earmarked for himself one day.

Later

Re-reading this I feel extremely mean and a real spoil-sport. Everyone had taken so much trouble in choosing presents and cards for me, and that made it so very special. The thing that hit me most of all was their love and the trouble they had taken in planning this day. I couldn't believe that Carol and little Timothy had actually travelled all this way just to be here and that they had actually managed to keep everything secret from me – amazing! Usually I know exactly what is going on despite all their efforts to conceal things.

It has made me feel really mean for not appreciating this birthday. I suppose that like so many family events it is just a wonderful excuse to celebrate and make the most of being together. In the end I found it was perfectly possible for me to enjoy the day, for their sake if not for my own. And anyway these days I guess it is quite a major achievement for a whole family still to be together after all this time – so let's be positive and make the most of the years we have left together.

George says that now perhaps I might understand a bit better why he felt so bad tempered about that big sixtieth party we held for him two years ago – and if I'm honest none of us really realized what he was feeling at the time. I suppose no one does until they actually get to this particular milestone.

Well at least I'm entitled to my free bus pass now and I'm certainly going to make the most of that! I think I shall also cash in on being able to become old and slightly batty, so that others can indulgently say, 'Oh well, there she goes again silly old bat.' Shall have to seriously consider what kind of eccentricity I want to go in for.... It reminds me of Jenny Joseph's wonderful poem:

When I am an old woman I shall wear purple,
With a red hat which doesn't go and doesn't suit me,
And I shall spend my pension on brandy and summer
    gloves,
And satin sandals and say we've no money for butter.
And I shall sit down on the pavement when I'm tired,
And gobble up samples in shops and press alarm
    bells
And run my stick along the public railings
And make up for the sobriety of my youth.
I shall go out in my slippers in the rain,
And pick the flowers in other people's gardens
And learn to spit.
You can wear terrible shirts and grow more fat
And eat three pounds of sausages at a go
Or only eat bread and pickles for a week

> And hoard pens and pencils and beermats and things
>   in boxes.[10]

What a wonderful picture of pure eccentricity – shall have to develop my own version of that!

Perhaps I could start with making sonorous comments under my breath during the sermon, and leaving rude notes on people's cars when they park too close to the house. And then I am sure I could find something suitably terrible and tatty to wear when some of our more fussy acquaintances come to visit. Oh yes, this has distinct possibilities!

It's quite a thought that not so many years ago most people would have been dead long before they reached this age – and this morning I might even have said 'And a good thing too!' Maybe I need to ask God what he wants me to do with however many years I have left, and to trust him with the future more than I have been doing to date.

> Even to your old age and grey hairs I am he, I am he who will sustain you. I have made you and I will carry you; I will sustain you and I will rescue you. (Isaiah 46:4)

18

Panic at First Babysitting Epic

Panic! Our first test case at babysitting Timothy without parental supervision, and to be honest I was absolutely terrified.

The trouble is we are both so wildly out of practice at all of this, and it matters so much more because he is our very first grandchild. His ever-trusting parents clearly expect us to be vastly more expert at looking after babies than either of us feels.

Carol handed him over with such complete confidence that I felt a total fraud. I can't remember the last time we looked after anyone's baby, besides which everything seems so terrifyingly different now.

Disposable nappies are wonderful, but I'm never quite sure I have pulled them tight enough at the waist to stay on and not leak, and Timothy wriggles around so that it's almost impossible to get any nappy back on at all!

Apparently these days it's quite okay for babies to be allowed to stay up half the night, to be fed whenever they want it and generally to be allowed to run the whole show.

After only a few hours of this non-existent routine

George could be heard muttering darkly about children being 'seen and not heard', and wanting to have his supper in peace without wailing children – and I have to confess that secretly I agreed with him!

But Timothy is so lovely, with those wonderful dark sorrowful eyes, that I'm afraid he could wind me round his little finger in no time. I expect he'll have to get a bit older before George takes any real interest in him – when he starts wanting to play with train sets or some kind of ball game.

Two days later

Absolutely exhausted! Can't imagine how I ever coped with *three* little ones. No wonder we have children when we are young enough!

End of the week – shattered!

Very sorry to see them go back to Scotland. It was so lovely to have the chance to spend enough time with them all and catch up on Carol's news – though she is very good at remembering to ring.

Peace at last – what absolute bliss! No more waking up to the sound of crying in the night, no more disturbed meals, no more chaos round the house. But goodness how I miss them now that they have gone!

Still finding myself listening out for Timothy's cheerful burbling, and wondering what he is doing now. Grandchildren are somehow so very special. Wish they lived a bit nearer. It feels as if Scotland is almost off the planet!

19

George Retires – Panic!

Hope that's not a bad omen – though it certainly feels like that! Good thing I'm not superstitious.

George finally retired yesterday evening amid a blaze of glory – need I say more?

The company gave him a wonderful send off, with speeches that could give him a swollen head for weeks. But listening to that litany of achievements only made me even more nervous about how he is ever going to survive a humdrum retirement in everyday suburbia, with nothing more important to get his mind around than whether anyone has fed the cat recently, or if the grass will need cutting today or tomorrow.

At least this morning he is still caught up in a warm glow following last night's celebrations and I honestly don't think reality has set in yet . . . perhaps I'll just give him time to find out for himself.

Being George of course he says he'll be 'fine', and no doubt he has rosy ideas of acres of time for golf and leisurely holidays driving round visiting friends. I also strongly suspect he has fantasies of lying out in the non-existent sun and reading the paper from cover to cover, rather as he used to imagine that I did whenever I wasn't officially 'working' – fat chance. Don't think he has the least idea how much of the day is gobbled up by boring things like washing up and weeding. But no doubt the office 'staff' would have had this efficiently in hand somewhere well out of his line of vision.

My trouble with George's retirement – and I feel a real heel for saying this – is that I actually used to quite enjoy having the house to myself when he went off in the morning, and being able to drift through the hours in my own sweet way. But now I have a nasty feeling that things will be very different once he is around all the time.

It probably sounds terrible because, although I really like the idea of having him here most of the time (I think!), he is so very much more organized than I am and absolutely loves to be able to plan out my whole life for me – giving me the benefit of his vast experience about exactly how everything should be done. But at least now, thanks to that seminar, I can remind him that as a spontaneous 'P' person myself I really can't cope with any of his 'J' organization – and that I really need to be left in peace to do it my way and in my own good time.

Whilst he was at work there was no need to disillusion him about how little difference his organization actually made to my life – since he was hardly ever there to witness the actual outcome of all his great 'plans' anyway. But now of course this will all be rather more obvious.

If the truth be told I never even think about what I am going to do next or exactly why and for what particular items I am going out shopping. So that when George expects me to give times and reasons for everything I do, it feels uncomfortably as if I am being attached to a collar and lead, which he may suddenly decide to rein in at a moment's notice.

I also quite like to pop out and visit friends up the road on impulse, without first having to make a programme or announce this beforehand, or tell him exactly what time I will be back.

Oh dear! I suppose this will all sort itself out in the end, but it looks rather choppy ahead on this particular stretch of water.

And then there's another thing about this retirement scene. For the past few weeks the telephone seems to have rung almost constantly with people besieging George to 'take on this' or 'organize that', 'now that he is going to have more time'. But in the end I have almost wanted to scream at them all: 'If he does everything you want him to do, then he simply won't have any time left! Why do you think he is retiring in the first place?'

Now we know why Jim and Elisabeth went off on an extended holiday the very day after he retired rather than allow Jim to get sucked into this local activity vortex. He said he needed time to make up his own mind what to do with all this newly acquired leisure, rather than just snatching at the very first thing that came along to shut out the emptiness. So it's really great that we shall have to be away for a good six weeks on this visit down under that George has planned to celebrate my birthday – perfect timing.

Obviously he does need something of value to do with his time, but I'm not at all sure that any of these things are really quite his scene. Sounds to me as if people in the parish have suddenly seen the opportunity to offload some of their own more boring or onerous responsibilities, without any real thought about whether or not these things are actually right for him.

According to Paul Tournier 'you really need to prepare for creative retirement several years beforehand' – but if that's true then there is not much hope for us! He reckons that 'most people are actually afraid of liberty, since we have all been brought up on the maxim "Work first play later"'.[11] Apparently one of his patients was such a slave to her work that in the end she found that nothing else gave her the feeling of really living. As a result she couldn't even begin to enjoy the longed for space of retirement because of the strange feeling of guilt that overcame her.

I wonder if that's the reason why so many retired people will take on almost any small insignificant job just in order to help them to feel useful members of society? It certainly seems odd that so many people find hobbies and interests that they have longed to pursue all their lives strangely less attractive once they actually have the time to pursue them.

I suppose it's true that some kind of routine feels much more comfortable to live with than uncharted emptiness, but the trouble is I have a sneaking feeling that God often speaks to us in that emptiness – if we actually have the courage to stop for a moment and listen to what he is saying.

I can't remember where I read it, but Catherine Doherty once said:

Stand still and allow the strange deadly restlessness of our tragic age to fall away like the worn out dusty cloak that it is – a cloak that was once considered beautiful. That restlessness was considered the magic carpet to tomorrow, but now in reality we see it for what it is: a running away from oneself, a turning from that journey inward that all men must undertake to meet God dwelling within the depth of their souls.

20
Valentine's Day

Sent George a Valentine's card this morning – as sober and masculine a picture as I could find, without all those hearts and roses. Always think it's quite a nice tradition, even if we are both getting a bit long in the tooth.

Amazing to think that there's only one more week to go before we get away to the sunshine and catch up with all our old friends again – can hardly believe it. The time has come round so quickly, and we're still frantically trying to make last minute arrangements: who is going to feed the cat, water the plants, deal with the answerphone, etc. Finding people to take on all our other commitments means lists, lists and more lists, and then in the end I lose the lists I made in the first place – hopeless! Just can't wait to get on that plane.

At this point George usually gets quite cranky and starts to ask whether going away is really worth all this effort beforehand! But there's absolutely no question in my mind. Probably he'd be perfectly happy just sitting here feeling 'settled' and 'organized' for the rest of his days if he didn't have me to unearth him and break up the routine a bit – and a good thing too I reckon!

I really hate these long dark days in February when

the winter seems never-ending and a sort of heaviness hangs in the air. So it's really wonderful to think of getting away from it all down under and not coming back till spring is well under way.

Jemima the cat is getting highly suspicious. She has this obsession about suitcases and knows instantly exactly what their appearance means.

Yesterday I found that she had packed herself neatly into the corner of George's and was trying to look especially appealing. The message was clear enough: 'Surely you couldn't possibly think of leaving me here all on my own could you?'

It makes me feel really mean of course – except that I know that the family who feed her while we are away will lavish her with attention, and take far more notice of her fussy eating habits than we do.

But no doubt she will turn her back on us when we return and really make us pay for the outrage of leaving her.

21

Seven Weeks Later

What a fantastic trip! But wonderful to be back in our own home again after six whole weeks of travelling.

Quite hard to think of settling down again to a whole new chapter of our lives officially in 'retirement'. But as for the mountains of mail on every available surface, and the jungle of weeds rapidly obliterating the garden after all that time away – the mind boggles! It really feels as if we will never ever catch up again.

I'm sure it was a brilliant idea to take a real break at this point in our lives, but it's strange how this sort of thing can really unsettle you. I suppose it's partly because there are so many wonderful friends we've had to leave behind and it was so hard to finally say 'good-bye'.

Still suffering with this unbelievable jet lag, and my whole body is just screaming at me, 'Sleep, sleep, please let me sleep.' But to be fair, it is still the middle of the night in Sydney. And it really doesn't help to come home to the gloom and the cold when we have just left behind brilliant sunshine, warm seas and a completely different kind of open air life.

No matter how hard we try we'll never be able to get

our world together – at least certainly not in this life. Suppose that's true for so many people we know, because in today's world there will always be friends and family on the other side of the globe. But just now we're still clinging tightly on to warm wonderful memories of people that we hadn't seen for ages – quite strange really.

When we first met up it felt as if nothing had changed and we had instantly travelled back six whole years in time as if it was only yesterday – the same lovely people, but all just a little bit older and hopefully wiser. And of course we remember them all exactly as they were when we were all living on that tiny tropical island together. But then before long you realize that every single one of us has really had to move on and change, because nothing in this world stays the same for ever.

Probably the strangest thing was the full realization that the little town where we had all lived out so many years of our life has just ceased to exist. The volcano has finally swallowed it up completely, leaving nothing but an ugly oozing mountain of mud and rubble, with only the occasional skeletal branch of a denuded palm tree or battered telegraph pole protruding above the heap.

I don't think either of us had fully realized just how total that destruction had been, until we saw some of the film from the Australian news coverage that our friends recorded at the time. Scanning the screen for some familiar landmark, some lone tree or rooftop that looked even remotely familiar, the horrible truth finally sank in . . . the little town where we had lived out five whole years of our lives had simply disappeared – except of course in our glorious technicolour memories of the most beautiful harbour in the South Pacific.

Often before I had felt this strange Armageddon-like

sensation whilst living in this spectacularly beautiful place. Sometimes I would look out at the smooth silken ocean where outrigger canoes plied their way gently out past the palm trees to the amazing coral reefs beyond, and at the time it seemed inconceivable that anything as drastic as a volcanic eruption could ever happen there – it was so serenely calm and beautiful.

I suppose it's a kind of parable about life and the fact that nothing on this planet lasts for ever. We just have to be thankful for the memories. None of us knows what this day or this year will bring. Life can just change in a flash, and without any warning we can lose so much that is precious.

Personally I found that this all focused my mind pretty effectively.

Because we lived for most of those years with the imminent threat of a volcanic eruption and with constant earthquakes, life on our island had a kind of wartime quality that older people so often talk about. Every morning the siren would sound for evacuation drill, and all the shops and offices were boarded up against a possible tidal wave. And as a result people of every nationality rallied together in a wonderful way.

Probably we got to know each other in ways that would be almost impossible in normal Western life today.

This started me thinking how lonely many people in our towns and villages are today, and how so much frantic busyness has taken over our world. No one seems to have time for other people any more, and so much of life consists of a sort of second-hand existence that is piped to us through television soap operas, or the advertising illusion that we can 'buy' happiness through out-of-town shopping malls or mail order catalogues – all of which can leave us feeling pretty empty and dissatisfied, without really knowing why.

Ultimately the search for intimacy is the search for God. Yet so many people are unaware of that truth. Instead they stop short at the search for intimacy itself. There is an insatiable thirst for deeper relationship, for greater encounter, for more complete marriages. Yet the search is a restless one and an uprooted one. The results are what we see around us in our broken society; damaged people with painful memories, moving from relationship to relationship to try to find one which will give them the depth of affirmation which their needy souls long for.[12]

It started me thinking about all those Bible promises of streams of living water flowing in the desert, and of Jesus saying to the woman at the well, 'Everyone who drinks this water will be thirsty again, but whoever drinks the water I give him will never thirst. Indeed, the water I give him will become in him a spring of water welling up to eternal life' (John 4: 13–14).

22
Paying for Our Absence

Jemima is still ignoring us, but managing to stand exactly midway between us and the fridge whenever we are in the vicinity, just in case we might possibly think of feeding her.

She is being very pointedly stiff and detached. . . . Clearly we have to atone for our departure first.

After that of course she will be all over us, and there will be no escape from her attentions – even to a sort of wailing in the night and the expectation that she absolutely must be allowed to sleep with us in case we manage to escape again.

At that point George usually takes pity on her and allows her into the bedroom. It's all right for him as he can usually sleep right through her attentions, but personally all I want is a bit of peace to get over my jet lag – and I definitely don't need her peering down into my face every half an hour or so during the night, just to make sure I am still there and haven't managed to escape. Why do we have pets?

23
George's First Official Week at Home in 'Retirement'

Monday

Woke up this morning to great thumping and puffing sounds from the bathroom next door. One of George's extra enthusiastic exercise routines was well underway, which of course immediately made me feel terribly guilty because I was still languishing in bed. Oh for a quiet life!

By breakfast time he was clearly feeling virtuous and elated. 'Well, what are we going to do today?' he demanded, obviously expecting me to have a complete schedule ready mapped out for him.

'Well . . . er,' I stuttered, completely taken aback by this unusually energetic start to a Monday morning, and sincerely trusting that this kind of thing was not going to become a habit!

'Perhaps we could just have a quiet cup of coffee and then go through the mail and sort of see how the day develops?'

Clearly this was not the response he wanted. His ever efficient secretary Joyce would obviously have had things much better planned out by now.

I was just thinking frantically about how on earth I was going to find time for all the housework and mess left over from our trip, *and* keep George happy now that we're home again, when mercifully the vicar rang to distract his attention.

Fortunately it proved to be a long and earnest consultation which just about gave me time to get my mind round a possible plan of action, but I honestly hope he is not going to carry on like this every morning, or I shall never be able to keep up the pace!

The trouble is that by no stretch of the imagination could one call George domesticated. He does occasionally wash up and do a bit of pruning, but apart from that. . . .

'What are we going to do?' usually means 'What are you planning to do, so that I can stand over you and give you the benefit of my valuable advice on how I think it should be done?'

To think that this is only 'day one' of the rest of our life together! How on earth am I going to survive the pace, I ask myself? I knew this wouldn't be easy, but obviously I underestimated the size of the problem. No wonder Majorie got herself in such a state last year when Fred retired. Poor woman – I just thought she was making a fuss about nothing and wasn't very sympathetic.

How on earth do I help him find enough interesting stimulating things to do without becoming his sort of permanent entertainment secretary? Or else leaving him to get swallowed up by demanding local needs? Or maybe I should just stay out of it and let him work this out for himself?

Anyway at that moment the doorbell rang and the shadow of Edith Oglethorpe appeared menacingly on the doorstep.

'I do hope you don't mind my dropping in?' This was clearly just a rhetorical question, since she elbowed her way determinedly straight past me into the hallway, totally satisfied in her own mind that we did not!

'Knowing that George is at home now I just thought I would take the opportunity to come round and give him the benefit of my opinion on what needs to be done in the graveyard,' she continued.

At times like this I can never understand why I am such a wimp and so unnecessarily polite!

I have to confess that Edith is definitely not my favourite person and I usually find myself ducking behind pillars and pews to avoid her whenever possible. She has all the qualities of a heat-seeking missile homing in on her target for the day. It's quite curious but she has a strange sort of squareness about her that I find very difficult to describe, and absolutely everything about her comes in varying shades of grey – with the exception of her very ruddy complexion which is also punctuated by piercing grey eyes.

Metal grey square glasses perch precariously on the very tip of her nose, and flat grey brogues carry her stubby frame purposefully in the direction of whoever she has in her sights – and absolutely nothing will be allowed to stand in the way! Rumour has it that the vicar lives in terror of her approaching shadow.

Oh dear, none of this sounds very Christian or charitable! I know she has her problems and I should be much more loving towards her. I suppose everyone has someone like this lurking on the sidelines of their lives and always ready to appear at all the most inauspicious moments. But right now Edith is definitely not what we need! It's ominous to say the least that she has realized on 'day one' that George is now retired, and therefore permanently 'available' to listen to her latest complaint. Sometimes they seem to be unending.

Found myself listening anxiously to see how he would cope.

And to my amazement it was barely ten minutes before I heard her being ushered purposefully back towards the front door.

'Thank you so much for coming,' he was saying in his best super-determined voice. 'It's always good to know what people in the parish think, and I am sure I shall be much better informed when the PCC discusses this next week, but in the meantime rest assured that we have the matter well in hand.'

So there was Edith looking slightly dazed walking back up the drive, clearly unsure of what had just hit her – not apparently at all offended but just shell shocked. Quite brilliant I reckon, and he did it all without hurting her feelings or making her feel unwelcome – amazing.

'Don't worry. I think she just needed someone to listen and make her feel a bit more important,' he said.

Clearly there's no need for me to worry about protecting George – and by the look of it he can teach me a thing or two! And I'm ashamed to say that he was much more loving than I would have been.

Not sure what an appropriate verse for today might be. I suppose this one just about says it all: 'A righteous man may have many troubles, but the Lord delivers him from them all' (Psalm 34:19).

24

Horrors of Visiting an Old People's Home

What an absolutely dreadful day! We'd been putting it off for weeks ever since we heard that Aunt Agatha had been moved to a home, but honestly I think that going to see her there was worse than even our most terrible imaginings. Apart from anything else it felt uncomfortably like shades of things to come, and left us both feeling seriously shaken.

'A goose walking over my grave' as my mother would have said.

Seeing all those old people just sitting round staring vacantly into space or gazing mindlessly at the TV was absolutely terrifying. And to think that they must all have lived active busy lives once upon a time, looking after families, and being valued members of some community!

Surely there must be something better for them than this?

We really must find somewhere nicer for her to go where she can be looked after properly and treated more like a human being and less like a member of the cabbage family. Please dear Lord don't let either of us end up like that.

Am going straight off to ring Joyce – she is such a

mine of information about this kind of thing. She was the first person to warn us about the dangers of moving out of the area when we retire – except for a very good reason, or with a view to being close to other friends. She has so many horror stories of people who can't wait to move down to the 'seaside' where they had those wonderful family holidays in the sunshine and instead end up with thousands of other sad old folk who have done exactly the same thing.

Those wonderful golden sands that they remembered for all the fun and enjoyment with the family in the prime of life now suddenly appear cold and empty with nothing but sad echoes and memories of a past that is gone for ever. The sun does not shine nearly as often as they remembered it, family and friends are miles away, and doctors' waiting lists are full to overflowing.

As we passed Portsmouth Docks and the sign saying 'to the Continent' we saw some wag had scrawled in graffiti under the name Bournemouth 'to the Incontinent', which seemed to sum up our feelings of a pretty depressing day fairly exactly.

Thank God we are not at that stage of life yet, but I suppose it's something we may well have to think about some day. Joyce told me to cheer up. It's not all that bad, and actually (according to her!) there are lots of wonderful homes if you know where to look.

Apparently there is an organization which will suggest exactly the right kind of place for you and help you to think through the issues – brilliant! I'm going to ring them first thing Monday morning and try to get Aunt Agatha moved as soon as possible.

I'm asking God never to let us get this old or this helpless – I really hope he will pull the plug before this; it's just too frightening a thought! Looked up one of my favourite passages in Isaiah to help me get all this into perspective and trust him with the future:

> Fear not, for I have redeemed you;
> I have summoned you by name; you are mine.
> When you pass through the waters,
> I will be with you;
> and when you pass through the rivers,
> they will not sweep over you.
> When you walk through the fire,
> you will not be burned;
> the flames will not set you ablaze.
> For I am the LORD, your God,
> the Holy One of Israel, your Saviour. (Isaiah 43:1–3)

If I am honest I know in my heart that he will never let anything happen to us without first giving us the strength to cope, but today was certainly a pretty nasty shock to the system.

> Oh Lord, let us not live to be useless, for Christ's sake.
>
> *John Wesley*

5 a.m. again

Goodness how I hate this time in the morning! What on earth is one supposed to do with the next three hours whilst the rest of the world sleeps? And then by the time they are all waking up bright eyed and bushy tailed, I am ready to drop and feeling as if I have already done a whole day's work.

When I am still lying in bed my head is full of wonderful ideas of things to write and paint ... but when I get up to do them they simply evaporate like the morning mist – hopeless!

25

Worrying about What We Are Going to Do

6th May

Woke up in the early hours again and started to think about what we are going to do with the rest of our lives – and got myself into quite a state worrying about this!

Perhaps all this was a result of rather a lot of cheese last night and too much in depth reading just before I went to sleep. Jung says:

> It is a law of life that it must always move forward. Not to take this forward step is to fail to see that to refuse to grow old is as foolish as to refuse to leave behind one's childhood. It is impossible to live through the evening of one's life in accordance with the programme appropriate to the morning, since what had the greater importance then will have very little now, and the truth of the morning will be the error of the evening. . . .
>
> What youth found to occupy himself in the world outside, man in the afternoon of his life must seek within himself . . . such riches will save him from boredom and give retirement its true meaning – not a withdrawal but an advance towards personal fulfilment.
>
> The man of more mature years experiences a press-

4

ing need for a more individual personal culture. An active person often allows many talents to lie fallow during working years and will need to rediscover spontaneity and originality, and to grasp intelligently the meaning of individual life.[13]

He goes on to say that to find the key to life and meaning in the later years we must recover those things that we really enjoyed as children but were drowned out by the 'oughts' of this world.

'It is a call', he says, 'to the fullness of life. How can you love and enjoy God in the next world if you cannot love and enjoy God in this world?' According to him, the rediscovery of the art of play is indispensable in the second half of life.

Well I certainly know that I need to find some kind of key! Most of the things I am still doing today are beginning to feel distinctly tired and dusty, and clouded out by a general lack of enthusiasm or inspiration, so maybe he is right.

Only a few weeks ago a very observant friend said to me, 'You know, nothing lights you up any more, Annabel. When you talk about what you are doing today there is no visible spark of interest or excitement like you had before.' At the time I wondered what on earth she was talking about, but now I think I am beginning to understand. The trouble is, she knows me too well!

Trying hard to remember the things that got drowned out in childhood. I know I used to get into terrible trouble for daydreaming when there was washing up to be done, and when all I wanted was to be left in peace to imagine wonderful happenings in the corridors of my mind. Given half a chance I could also while away hours and hours in the school studio, painting endless sunsets without even noticing how the time simply flew past.

Whenever I see paintings in a shop window or visit an exhibition, I feel a sudden thrill of excitement and a longing to get out the paint brushes again – though I seem to have so little time these days.

But it's so frustrating that as soon as the urge to paint strikes then I will remember with a sinking heart that horrible pile of ironing overflowing the basket. I do so hate all these beastly monotonous jobs! No matter how hard I try they are always there, lurking somewhere in the background of life.

Why do I feel so guilty about allowing myself any time to sit down and paint? The Protestant work ethic has a lot to answer for I reckon! If you are in danger of enjoying anything then it must by definition be wrong. 'No time to play until your work is finished' – which quite frankly in my book means 'never'!

And if this is difficult for me then it must be so much harder for someone like George. His whole world seems to be full of oughts and duties, and sometimes I just long to be able to dig him out from under the heap.

And I'm really not sure what all this 'seeking riches within himself' might mean for him. If I ever mention this then I'm sure he will just make fun of the whole idea. I suppose the only way is to wait until he actually recognizes the need to escape from it all.

Anyway I think I shall put up a notice above the sink saying 'Look inside', just to remind me not to get bogged down in domesticity. Probably George will think the drains need unblocking or something, but that's just too bad!

Found myself reading Henri Nouwen again and his wonderful words 'In search of Meaning':

'What am I doing and for what reason?' lurks beneath all of our good feelings about family, friends and work. . . . Is this really our world, our people, our existence? What is everyone so busy with?

The question comes from a place deeper than emotions, feelings or passions. It is the question about the meaning of existence raised not just by the mind, but also by a searching heart. A question that makes us feel like strangers in our own milieu. People take on a robot like quality. They do many things but don't seem to have an interior life. Some outside power seems to wind them up and make them do what they are doing.

Without a deep sense of belonging, all of life can easily become cold, distant, and painfully repetitive. This deeper connection is the connection with the one whose name is love, leading to a new discovery that we are born out of love and are always called back to that love. It leads to a new realization that God is the God of life who continues to offer us life wherever and whenever death threatens. It ultimately leads to prayer. And from our being human . . . comes a new experience of being held within the hand of a loving God.[14]

4.30 a.m.

Oh no! The trouble is I'm wide awake now, but by 7 a.m. I shall be like a zombie! What is one supposed to do at this time of night and before dawn has even broken? I suppose it might be a good time to paint, but thinking about the warm bed I have just left has a pretty strong pull. Perhaps I'll just slip back inside the covers for a while and hope I drop off.

26
George Is Getting into Computers

14th May

I can't believe it! George, who has never done a day's typing in his life, is actually learning to use the computer and what is more he's getting really enthusiastic about this – amazing! If anyone had told me a few months ago that this would happen I would simply have laughed in their face.

Watching him bent double over the keyboard, bashing furiously away with two fingers and totally absorbed in what he is doing is really an incredible sight. And the great thing from my point of view is that this means he will actually be wanting to type all his own letters now – brilliant!

But this whole 'computer babble' language is really something. He rattles away to Richard about 'modems' and 'rams' and is apparently now seriously thinking of 'logging on to the net' so that he can download things – the mind boggles!

Listening with half an ear it sounds rather like some kind of fishing accident that went badly wrong.

Being George of course he does the thing in style, reads all the books and magazines, talks to all the experts and even goes to the computer shows. And then comes back loaded with all kinds of remarkably useless gadgets and additions that I can't see that he is ever going to use.

But never mind – it's really proving a wonderful hobby for him and is keeping him very busy. Honestly this is just what the doctor ordered as a new skill to learn in retirement. Considering that he is almost totally untechnical this is something I would *never* have expected him to get enthusiastic about in a million years.

I read somewhere that this is fast becoming the most popular hobby for men in retirement, and a really exciting up-to-the-minute challenge for the little grey cells.

It's wonderful for me because whenever my computer refuses to do what it is told (i.e. frequently) all I have to do is summon George to the rescue and he knows almost immediately what is wrong.

He simply loves poring over all the manuals and (unlike me) he starts at the very beginning and plods through from page to page, so that he knows exactly what to do from day one. Whereas personally I always jump straight in to the page that interests me – leaving out all the bits in between – until I get massively stuck and have to ask for help yet again.

Amazing how our different personalities show up in every corner of life!

27

Fed up with My Fellow Wrinklies

Such a relief to spend the day with someone whose only preoccupation was not retirement and the state of their pension fund. . . .

Honestly it sounds very critical but sometimes I can hardly cope with some of my fellow 'wrinklies', who seem to be totally stuck in a rut. They don't even appear to want to look up and see that there's a lot more to life out there – even at our age. After all we're not dead yet. . . .

What brought all this gloom and doom on I wonder?

I think it must have been that visit out of the blue yesterday from James and Fiona whom we used to know so well when they lived down the road. I'm sure he is only a couple of years older than George, but talking to them yesterday it felt as if they were closer to a hundred and positively galloping towards their dotage.

I could hardly bear to listen to some of the things they were saying, it was all so pointless and depressing – and all about packing up and letting go. The only thing on their minds seemed to be moving to a smaller place, doing less and less, and generally sliding gracefully into a comfortable early decline. But the frightening thing to me was that they had only just acquired their free bus passes! I just hate to think what they will be like in five or ten years' time if they are still around.

I suppose he always just lived for his job, and they have neither of them any other outside interests or concerns for the community around them, or for that matter any real faith. James used to call himself a scientific atheist, and Fiona always just followed dutifully in his footsteps, repeating whatever he said. It's a pity they don't live closer – so difficult to help when they are miles away.

Anyway today it was just wonderful to be around some younger people again and to feel recharged by the spin off from their energy. It actually started me doing a quick calculation and realizing rather guiltily that quite a few of the friendships I now value are those with considerably younger people – just hope they don't see me as some old bat whom they have to humour and tolerate!

I wonder if there's some kind of relay switch that turns off automatically in some people's brains when they get to a certain age? A sudden need to reach for the cotton wool and the TLC, and a longing for nothing more than to sit quietly in the sunlight and watch the shadows lengthen.

It's really quite a difficult juggling act to get this right I reckon. Physically we can't do as much as we used to, and we are certainly already getting close to the slippery slope, but then surely that doesn't mean we have to become this inward looking and self-protective? Surely we must have a great deal more to offer people?

'Is not wisdom found among the aged? Does not long life bring understanding?' (Job 12:12).

'You are old at any age', says John Eddison, quoting from the Minnesota Medical Association,

If. . . .
You feel you have learnt all there is to learn;
You find yourself saying 'I'm too old for that';
You feel tomorrow holds no promise;
You take no interest in the activities of youth;
You would rather talk than listen;
You long for 'the good old days', feeling they were best.[15]

I still remember my mother-in-law being absolutely up to the minute about everything that was going on around her long after she had entered her seventies. Those wonderful letters she used to write to me when we were living abroad, to keep me up to date with all that very practical information, such as the length of skirts people were wearing and what the fashion would be like when we got home (quite necessary after all those years out in the sticks). And I'll never forget her coming to a company party when she was in her eighties and just longing to be asked to join in and dance.

The chairman appeared to be quite shocked – as if in old age he expected a bit more decorum!

It's really amazing how people vary as they grow older, and clearly some are much more ready to adapt to change than others who seem to cling like drowning swimmers to how things always used to be in the 'good old days'.

Yesterday I found this lovely quotation from George Congreve:

I find growing old something quite new and a surprise. I feel it is a sort of undressing of the soul for the next and better stage of our journey. I am so sure of the purpose of God for us, an increasing purpose from good to better, that I determine not to notice even in my thoughts (if I can help it) the inconveniences and absurdities, the mortifications that come with the years. We are not at home in them, only pushing on through them on the way home.[16]

28
Red Letter Day

What a wonderful day. And totally unexpectedly out of the blue which always makes it so much more special.

I was just contemplating the pile of washing up in the sink and all the depressing things that assail one after a frantically busy weekend, when George galloped in like a white knight to the rescue.

'Oh don't let's bother with all that now,' he said firmly. 'Come on, it's a wonderful day outside, and who cares if it's Monday? Why don't we go and explore that nice looking walk in the hills above Godalming that we saw last week?'

'Well ... I really ought to get the place straight ...' I began, when he stopped me in mid sentence with that wonderful quizzical look over the top of his glasses.

'Who was talking about enjoying life and getting away from the "oughts"?' he enquired innocently. 'It will be so much easier to handle when we get back, and you'll feel much better for it.'

So we just shut the door on it all and drove off into the Surrey hills, bent on nothing more than enjoying ourselves and drinking in the glorious spring colours – wonderful! The trees were bursting out in all directions with those brilliant fresh green satin leaves. There was an absolute carpet of primroses and celandine under the willows by the stream, and the air seemed almost aglow with supercharged electricity.

We walked for a good two hours over the hills beyond Guildford with a patchwork of fields spread out below us and tractors like tiny toys marking out patterns in the soil far below us. We could easily have been a million miles away and I forgot all about home and chores, absolutely what I needed.

The best Monday I have had for years. Our first red letter day of George's retirement – and hopefully a herald of many more days to come!

Tuesday

Just heard that Carol and Tony are coming down to stay with us next week – wonderful! This is really turning out to be a brilliant week after all my misgivings. It will be so lovely to catch up with them and to see Timothy again.

Help! Have just realized that the spare room is a major tip after all the chaos of last week's jumble sale – will have to get the place sorted ASAP!

At present we are on the outside of the world, the wrong side of the door. We discern the freshness and purity of morning, but they do not make us fresh and pure. We cannot mingle with the splendours we see. But all the leaves of the New Testament are rustling with the rumour that it will not always be so. Some day, God willing, we shall get in.

C S Lewis[17]

29

The Dreaded Subject of Money

On EEEEEEEEs and pensions and all that

Goodness how I hate the subject of money!

Last night just before bedtime we got onto the whole depressing subject of pensions and interest rates and how little we are going to have to live off, and as a result I seem to have spent the whole night wallowing like a hippopotamus in a quagmire of rumpled sheets.

I know it's true that interest rates on our savings are falling like a stone. Which of course may be a very good thing for those people with mortgages, but for us oldies it's a pretty gloomy prospect. Personally I just try not to think about this kind of thing too much.

Nothing fills me with more despair than 'budgeting' for our future – which effectively seems to mean working out that we can't afford to do anything we really want to do. Why is it that we work all our lives struggling to earn a reasonable income and then when we finally have the time to enjoy life a bit there isn't enough money to do what we want to do anyway?

I don't think I'll ever understand the finer points of finance, and I'm sure that George is just being super cautious, but honestly that sort of thing just before one goes to bed is really dire . . . and completely off limits.

Unfortunately, like for most men, it's really meat and drink to him, and he doesn't feel happy until he has worked out exactly what we've got.

Personally I just like to trust God with the future and believe that he will look after us. He has never let us down yet. But to George that sounds as if I am burying my head in the sand and being very irresponsible. I suppose that probably we will never see eye to eye on this.

Therefore I tell you, do not worry about your life, what you will eat; or about your body, what you will wear. Life is more than food, and the body more than clothes. Consider the ravens: They do not sow or reap, they have no storeroom or barn; yet God feeds them. And how much more valuable you are than birds! Who of you by worrying can add a single hour to his life? Since you cannot do this very little thing, why do you worry about the rest? (Luke 12:22–26)

If I could live in a tiny dwelling on a rock in the ocean, surrounded by the waves of the sea and cut off from the sight and sound of everything else, I would still not be free of the cares of this passing world or from the fear that somehow the love of money might come and snatch me away.

Cuthbert of Lindisfarne

5 a.m. again

So looking forward to Carol and Tony arriving tomorrow, and especially to seeing how Timothy has grown – I can hardly wait! He is nearly seven months now.

30
Why Do I Feel So Tired?

16th June

It was so lovely seeing Timothy again and having them all staying here, but am feeling absolutely exhausted this morning. Just can't believe all the things I used to do and don't seem to have the energy for any more.

Made the mistake of mentioning this fact to George and got told that all I needed was a bit more exercise to increase my stamina – great! So helpful. . . .

Suppose if I'm honest he is probably not far off the mark, but then he doesn't have all this washing and ironing and cleaning to do. Perhaps I should suggest he does his next morning routine with the hoover in tow.

The trouble is I really hate all those meaningless exercises – even though I do usually feel better afterwards – but not until quite a long time afterwards!

Bumped into our old doctor last week, who fixed me with his steely glare and asked rather pointedly how much exercise I was getting. Surely it can't be that obvious?

'You need three good bursts of proper exercise a week,' he said, ignoring my protestations completely. 'And I don't want to hear about how tired you are, because that only makes it even more necessary. None of this couch potato nonsense now.'

Don't think much of his bedside manner, but suppose I shall have to take some notice of what he says. Trouble is, it's all so boring. Perhaps I could form a sort of exercise club and get some friends together to make the time pass a bit more quickly and painlessly?

Can just imagine how rude George would be about this, and no doubt it would acquire some dreadful title such as 'The Female Elephants Club'.

NB Not going to let this deter me – think it might make this whole exercise thing much easier for all of us.

31

Old Friends Moving Away

A *really black* day today – Irene and John moving down to Cornwall.

I wonder how many more of our very old friends are going to move away leaving us marooned here in suburbia? Two bits of driftwood abandoned on the sand when the tide has gone out.

Could hardly bear watching them load that enormous removal van with all their familiar possessions and realizing that they won't be there any more to drop in for a cup of tea or to have a quiet natter. Irene has been such an absolute gem of a friend, always available for everyone and never too busy. Can't imagine how the neighbourhood will cope without her, never mind how we will.

I'm worried about her as well. John has always been so keen to move out to the country as soon as he retired, and this grand plan has been in the pipeline for years. I suppose we all just hoped it wouldn't happen when the time actually came. But then John has never been easily diverted from his aims in life (another 'J' I suppose).

I'm sure Irene is a lot more upset than she is admitting. Could see she was almost in tears seeing everything being packed up and realizing that the time to go had finally come. She only coped up to then by putting the whole thing at the back of her mind and concentrating on the positive. I gather that John had simply insisted that this was what they had always planned for – end of subject. He is absolutely sure that she will love Cornwall when they have settled in. I just hope he's right.

Still I have to admit that the pictures of the new home look simply wonderful – a lovely old farmhouse with grounds running down to the sea, and a whole mass of rambling outbuildings. I gather the place needs a great deal of work, but the theory is that 'it will give John something to do' in his retirement.

George says he just hopes he will enjoy it when the time comes – because he can't think of anything worse!

After their wonderfully comfortable home here it's all going to be quite a shock to the system, and anyway John's DIY has always been something of a nightmare to live with. Irene had everything so beautifully organized and decorated here. Oh well, just watch this space and pray that they will be okay. We've promised to go and stay with them as soon as they are settled.

Can hardly face looking at the empty house and wishing they were still around.

5 a.m. again

Found myself rolling around in bed and shivering because George had managed to acquire most of the duvet. Quite a relief actually, as I was in the middle of a horrible dream about having to move to some ghastly derelict hovel with spiders' webs draped everywhere, rats playing football in the basement, and rotten floorboards that we kept falling through. George apparently had wonderful plans to turn the place into some kind of health farm. Mercifully in the cold light of dawn even I can see that this is an extremely unlikely scenario!

Started thinking about the perpetual question that strikes one at this time of life: 'to move or not to move'.

Without a particular reason to go we had finally come to the conclusion that it was right to stay put . . . until Irene and John decided to go. The trouble is, every time something like this happens it always unsettles us yet again, and then I start wondering if there will be anyone left here to come and visit us when we are in our dotage.

Our children and friends seem to be scattered in all directions north, south, east and west of here, and it just seems impossible to even think of moving away ourselves. The trouble is that being closer to some people would inevitably mean being even further away from others, so we really can't win.

It's amazing how many older people make the mistake of moving just to be closer to their children when they will be totally and solely dependent on them, without realizing that they may well be posted to Timbuctoo or Sydney, or at the very least some distant corner of this country. And sometimes I can't help wondering if the children really want their parents that close anyway.

A couple of years ago when we thought Carol and Tony might just possibly have settled in Dorset we considered moving further down in that direction, where we have quite a few friends already, but now that they've upped and moved to Scotland there really isn't much point. I suppose at the end of the day travel is an awful lot easier when you live near London. And since two of our 'children' live there (or at least they do at present), we will still be able to see something of them.

But every summer when we go out to visit friends in the depths of the country it seems increasingly hard to come back to suburbia. And then we start having second thoughts again about moving – hopeless.

And then I find myself thinking of friends who moved away several years ago and yet keep on coming back to visit because all their real friends are still here, and it all seems a bit pointless.

NB Need to trust God with this whole problem, and believe that he will show us if it's time to move.

Am going to make myself a cup of tea and then go back to bed to reclaim my share of the duvet.

I have learned the secret of being content in any and every situation, whether well fed or hungry, whether living in plenty or in want. I can do everything through him who gives me strength. (Philippians 4:12–13)

The Land of Lost Content

Into my heart an air that kills
From yon far country blows:
What are those blue remembered hills,
What spires, what farms are those?

This is the land of lost content,
I see it shining plain,
The happy highways where I went
And cannot come again.

A E Housman[18]

32

Trying to Pretend We Weren't Still in Bed

Now that George doesn't have to catch the train at some unbelievably early hour every morning, we quite often find ourselves climbing out of bed later and later, which is really nice – until the milkman rings the doorbell, or one of the neighbours has some urgent request.

It's so embarrassing trying to look vaguely alert and ready for the world, without having to admit that we have only just got out of bed.

'No, really – you haven't actually woken us up – I always read the paper in my dressing gown first thing; do a bit of hoovering before I get dressed; water the plants first, etc., etc. . . .'

I doubt very much if they are remotely convinced by this, but at least it makes me feel better.

I always wondered why so many of our retired friends seemed so switched off first thing in the morning, but am rapidly beginning to understand this syndrome!

Goodness it seems only a few months ago that I was still getting up at 6 a.m. every day – what on earth has happened to me? Nowadays even when I do wake up at the crack of dawn, all I want to do is snuggle back down again under the duvet. And I must admit it's really nice having George sleeping soundly beside me, instead of shaving away furiously next door and drowning out whatever I was trying to listen to on the radio.

I think he is getting comfortably used to this way of life as well, which is lovely to see. Of course he's still pretty busy – as in fact we both are – but now he can be heard laughingly telling other people that he's no idea how he ever found time to go to work.

Extraordinary how work expands to the space you allow it – basic Parkinson's Law I guess. When I think back to how much we both used to cram into a single day it's really quite frightening. So good not to have to live every day at breakneck speed any more. In fact I think we're really beginning to quite enjoy this retirement thing despite all our misgivings.

Have noticed how relaxed George seems to be all of a sudden. He is laughing much more and obviously enjoying lots of little things that I remember he used to like doing when we first got married. I'm only just beginning to realize what terrible pressure his job was putting him under, and how lovely it is to rediscover the man I first married under the heap.

But the trouble is that with all this relaxing we're getting later and later – which is fine, or at least it would be, if I didn't feel so guilty!

This morning we were really both of us seriously late. George was late for his Housing Association meeting in Godalming, and I had completely forgotten we had asked the Joneses to lunch – and that there was hardly anything left in the fridge. Obviously we are going to have to get ourselves just a bit more organized!

But it's really great to have a bit more time for other people at last, and not to be constantly looking over our shoulders at that pile of work on the desk or messages on the answerphone. It's surprising how many people seem to need a listening ear and someone just to be there for them. Difficult to get this down as a job description of course, but honestly does it matter? I believe God sends us those people he wants us to see, and if we can help them so much the better.

And perhaps the most important thing of all is to take time to pray for them – which again has often been completely drowned out by lack of time. It knocked me sideways the other day when Betty told me that she prayed for me every day! I had absolutely no idea and it really moved me to discover this.

33

A Brilliant Sunny Day with My Paints

Another brilliantly sunny day, but unfortunately George had to go to a meeting for one of his housing charities.

Inspired by his encouragement and good example a while ago, I decided to make the best of the opportunity, ignored the washing up, the ironing and even the state of the kitchen cupboards and went in search of my paints instead. Quite proud of myself!

Ridiculous how I almost felt like a naughty child doing this – at sixty for goodness sake! But I'm determined to work on this inner life and creativity that Jung was talking about. For ages I've been longing to give myself time to paint, but instead I've let myself be held back and almost imprisoned by meaningless chores. Enough of this! Especially now that George has set me such a great example!

Got out my watercolours (a bit dried out and dusty but still more or less usable) and found myself a nice sunny spot at the back of the house where we just get a view of the downs in the distance when it's clear. Spent a wonderful morning trying out lots of different washes for the sky and then adding distant hills and trees and plants in the foreground.

Needless to say the finished product was nothing like the original – nor for that matter like the brilliant masterpiece that existed in my head; that is to say, before it got put down on paper. But I spent an absolutely wonderful day lapping up the sunshine with all of God's creation spread out before me.

Had never noticed before how quickly the light changes and the clouds roll across the sky. It's almost impossible to get it all down in time before the whole scene moves on again. The different golds and reds in the autumn trees and shrubs are just breathtaking.

As I was sitting so quietly all kinds of creatures emerged from the shadows: tiny birds scavenging for insects in the lawn, foxes just making themselves at home in our garden and using the pond as a drinking bowl, and dozens of bumble bees searching for pollen in the last of the flowers on the rockery.

The day seemed to go like a flash, and the strange thing was that I felt totally at peace with myself and far more in touch with God and his creation than I have done for weeks. It was almost as if he wanted me to come apart and listen to his heartbeat in the beauty he had created. Perhaps that sounds fanciful, but I felt his love and his closeness in a new and wonderful way.

NB Definitely going to paint more often and take time to drink in the beauty God has made for us to enjoy.

In seedtime learn, in harvest teach, in winter enjoy.

William Blake

What is this life, if full of care,
We have no time to stand and stare.

William Henry Davies

34

Madelaine's Funeral

Madelaine's funeral today. Very sad, but also a service threaded through with moments of joy and delightful memories. Lots of people I hadn't seen for years came flooding back for the occasion. Goodness, there's nothing like this sort of event for making you realize how old we are all getting.

I really like the way our vicar gets people in the congregation to stand up and talk about their special memories of the person who has died, and it's amazing what people actually share. It almost felt as if Madelaine lived and walked among us again, and we were able to have a quiet chuckle together about some of her funny little ways.

Sometimes she used to forget where she was going, and follow people coming out of the first service when she had only just arrived herself, so that the vicar had to gently steer her back again saying, 'Wouldn't you like to stay for the service now that you have come?'

Often she would keep very charmingly introducing herself to the same people on every occasion she met them. But also in her later years, and after quite a high flown academic career, she had been rediscovering a wonderful childlike sense of humour and fun. When she was younger apparently her sheer intellect and fierce bright eyes sometimes easily frightened people who came across her. Not a few of them admitted to me after the service that they had been scared stiff of her in the beginning. But by the time we knew her she was just a rather lovely old lady with a tremendous sense of fun.

Maybe that's why we need our later years so that we can recover our sense of joy and wonder in life – to rescue the child that God created from beneath the heap of life's problems and worries? Truly our second childhood in more ways than one.

At ninety-five Madelaine was getting a bit absent-minded and more than a little blind and deaf as well, but she kept her sense of humour right up to the end and could laugh at her own infirmities. I can remember her feeling around in one of her copious cupboards to find and show us a painting she had done when she could still see properly – but there was no sense of self-pity, and she just seemed to trustingly accept what had happened to her.

Her grandson talked about what a wonderful letter writer she had been, never forgetting for a single week. On one occasion a letter arrived in the most extraordinary almost illegible handwriting. It turned out that her wrist was in plaster after quite a bad break, but never daunted, she had gone on to write the letter with her other hand, finding the whole experience excruciatingly funny: 'I bet you can't tell who this letter is from,' she taunted him.

Someone else spoke of the last few years of her life in the nursing home many miles away from here. When her family went to visit her she would sometimes have that faraway look on her face and be quietly laughing to herself – and then they knew she had been 'travelling' again. 'Chasing camels again out in the desert actually,' she said, laughing.

Extraordinary how far back one goes in old age – just as if all the wonderful experiences of our lives are recorded in full glorious technicolour to come back and delight us when we most need them.

Perhaps the most moving thing was the quality and certainty of her faith. She believed and trusted absolutely in God and knew without a doubt that she was on her way to be with him

They had chosen one of my favourite readings for the funeral, and at long last I found out who wrote it:

I said to the man who stood at the gate of the year, 'Give me a light that I may tread safely into the unknown.'

And he replied, 'Go out into the darkness and put your hand into the hand of God. That shall be to you better than light and safer than the known way.'

So I went forth, and finding the hand of God, trod gladly into the night. And he led me towards the hills and the breaking of the day in the East.

Minnie Louis Haskins

8 a.m.

The sunrise this morning was a really special brilliant gold with purple blotches all over the sky, and well worth being conscious for.

Just thinking again about 'memories' and why it is that events which happened years and years ago seem

to return in such brilliant technicolour in old age –
almost as if people are actually travelling backwards in
time.

I love that African saying that must have come from
riding along their incredibly bumpy potholed roads:
'What gets put onto the lorry first stays on board until
the very end of the journey.'

35

The Shock of Seeing Contemporaries Again After So Many Years

Started thinking again about all our contemporaries getting older. It is often a real shock to see people again after ten or twenty years' absence, and realize uneasily that if they are looking much older then we probably are too, it's just that we don't always recognize this.

Duncan looked so old and bent, as if all the troubles of the world had been heaped upon his shoulders. Poor thing. He really must have been through the mill with all those months of unemployment and then losing his wife in that accident. It was almost impossible to believe that he is barely two years older than George.

I am sure George is looking older these days as well, but the grey streaks in his hair and the added circumference just make him look more comfortable and more distinguished – or at least I think they do. Quite nice really, especially when he peers at me over the top of his glasses in that quizzical way.

Age is not all decay. It is the ripening, the swelling of fresh life within, that withers and bursts the husk.

George Macdonald

36
Black Holes

So embarrassed this morning I just didn't know where to put myself!

I bumped into this couple down in town whom I've known for absolutely years, but couldn't for the life of me remember their names.

I was getting along quite nicely despite this, whilst frantically racking my brain for some kind of clue – calling them 'you' in a really friendly way, and asking vague detached sort of questions like 'How are your children doing these days?', and generally trying to sound as if I knew what I was talking about, as you do – when to my absolute horror Jane came bounding up, clearly expecting to be introduced.

In a moment of panic I clutched desperately at the first words that came into my head: 'I suppose you have met?'

When they both denied this point blank, quite naturally turning to me to enlighten them, I proceeded to make an absolute fool of myself, flannelling away pathetically like some kind of gibbering idiot, and no doubt turning bright red in the process.

'This is . . . er . . . goodness . . . I am sure I really know your names – they just seem to have completely slipped my mind. How very extraordinary!'

They did their best to get me out of the hole I had dug for myself of course, but it was obvious from the rather stiff way they proceeded to introduce themselves that they were both quite offended ... probably felt they should have been completely unforgettable. And let's face it I have known them long enough!

I didn't know where to put myself. Honestly if I am going to go on like this I don't know where it will end. Talk about galloping senility!

Jane was very sensible about it. 'Oh don't worry,' she said cheerfully. 'I just call them black holes – everyone has them at our age. You know – suddenly something you know perfectly well just evaporates into thin air, and no matter how hard you try you can't get it back. At least, not until long after you really needed it in the first place.'

'Black hole' is a pretty good description I reckon, but how is it possible to forget the name of someone you have known well for twenty odd years? No trouble with the face, but a complete blank with names, however desperately one searches through the mental filing system.

Decided I will have to evolve some kind of foolproof technique for avoiding this kind of crunch situation in the future. How about the American ploy of 'Do introduce yourselves', as if you know perfectly well who they are, but think that they will perform this task better than you can?

Or perhaps one could try rattling on enthusiastically, 'This is an old friend of ours we have known for years,' and just hang in there long enough, hoping that they will fill in the gaps for you before you have to admit the grizzly truth.

But thinking about this afterwards, the really annoying thing is that even if you do manage to introduce them with the utmost finesse and get their names exactly right, you know perfectly well that they will all have completely forgotten these again in a matter of minutes . . . but such is life!

There is a wicked inclination in most people to suppose an old man decayed in his intellects. If a young or middle aged man upon leaving a company does not recollect where he laid his hat it is nothing. But if the same inattention is discovered in an old man, people will shrug their shoulders and say 'His memory is going.'

Dr Johnson

Apparently my father-in-law (who was old enough to have been George's grandfather) made a whole speech at George's twenty-first birthday party, in which it quickly became obvious that he had completely mistaken him for his younger brother. And whenever he called any of the children he would simply string all their names together, knowing that this way he would get at least one of them right.

Oh well, I haven't quite got to that stage yet, but I'm clearly going to have to do something drastic about this whole memory thing.

37

End of the Christmas Break — Absolutely Exhausted!

I don't seem to have had a minute to write anything in this book for weeks – and it doesn't feel as if I've had much chance to *sit down* in all those weeks either.

It was so lovely to have the whole family staying here for Christmas, but those unending meals often felt like stocking a huge overladen conveyor belt with enough food to feed an army. And even then, no sooner had we finished one meal than there would always be someone else asking what was for supper. Can't imagine how I managed to feed them all when they lived here all the time! I suppose I had a bit more energy then.

But so lovely to have Timothy here and to watch his excited little face at the sight of the lighted Christmas tree. Somehow it was like seeing Christmas all over again through completely new eyes – although I know he is still really too young to begin to understand what it's all about or to appreciate the crib down at the church.

After all our careful wrapping up of his presents, it was crystal clear that by far the greatest fun consisted of ripping off all the paper as quickly as possible, and then going on to the next one to do the same. I'm sure he would have been just as happy with a whole lot of well-wrapped empty boxes covered in brightly coloured paper and string! There must be a lesson there somewhere.

One afternoon we took him down to Salisbury and as we were walking back with him in the pushchair towards the cathedral car park at dusk, he suddenly caught sight of the lighted tower and just sat there spellbound for ages gazing up at it in the sky high above him. You could almost imagine his little voice saying 'Wow!'

How easy it is to lose sight of the wonder of childhood!

38

How Important Can You Be?

Still suffering from that really boring evening yesterday with those rather pompous new neighbours from down the road, Commander and Mrs Entwhistle.

I am sure that between them they spent the entire evening banging on and on about all the very important jobs he had once held, each story getting more boring and more pointless than the last, as if their very survival depended on our recognizing his former brilliance.

'When my husband was awarded this medal, when he was mentioned in Dispatches, when he was summoned to Buckingham Palace . . .' It seemed to go on forever, like some kind of litany . . . and the sad thing was that basically neither of us really needed to know all this, and I don't suppose we were looking suitably impressed.

It was actually all getting terribly embarrassing, and I didn't dare even look at George in case his expression gave me the giggles. He absolutely hates this kind of thing and is apt to put on his special artificially pompous look for the occasion. I just hope they didn't realize what he was doing.

You can't help feeling sorry for them really. I suppose

that like so many people they've never learnt how to just be themselves without all those titles and past medals. If only they knew that we would have been perfectly happy just to accept and befriend them just as they are without all this paraphernalia!

It was all actually quite unnerving – because suddenly I could almost hear those startling words from Isaiah echoing in my mind as she was speaking: 'All men are like grass, and all their glory is like the flowers of the field. . . . The grass withers and the flowers fall, but the word of our God stands for ever' (Isaiah 40:6, 8).

It's a bit sad really, as obviously they don't feel of any real value in themselves, and think that we will be more impressed by all this, without realizing how much it actually drives people away. I gather the Country Club positively rattles with people like this, all jostling to tell each other how important they once were – whereas in reality no one wants to know.

Started thinking about this afterwards. I suppose status and reputation are all part of what we have to pack up and put away in later life – rather like grandfather's medals stowed away in leather boxes in the attic. Few people remember the events or the battles any more, and we only really treasure them because they remind us of him, rather like his old battered carpet slippers and stripy dressing gown.

Decided what's really important is what we're like on the inside – the real essential kernel of our identity, the bit we so often keep locked, bolted and barred in the cellar. It's those funny little things that matter so much to us, the really special experiences that make our faces light up and come alive again.

Decided to be completely honest with myself (which is always very therapeutic!) and look at what is really important to me at this stage of life. In the end I concluded that it does all come down to 'people'.

Friends and family are really the most priceless possessions that I have accumulated along the great highway of life. But then carelessly I so often forget about them and allow them to be crowded out of my diary and overgrown with the weeds of busyness – until they move away or die suddenly, and then I am overcome with remorse and regret.

Friends I've known and loved for a very long time are the most precious of all. Their presence resonates with the memory of experiences we have shared together – sometimes even quite painful traumatic ones that were once the source of major disagreements, now long since forgotten. These tried and tested friends that we have really been through the mill with are like gold dust. They are warm and comfortable to be with, like well-worn favourite shoes that will accompany us safely through the storms ahead. . . .

Reading Paul Tournier last night I found it fascinating that he was writing about the same kind of thing. He calls this the 'medicine of the person'.

We need people who will devote themselves to the poverty of our personal relationships. . . . I see the old have a real job to do. It is a terribly important one: the restoration to our impersonal society of the human warmth, the soul that it lacks. When we are young we have to build our careers, and carve out a place in society for ourselves. Later on the career absorbs more and more of our time and energy. We have little time to take any interest in the persons of others. We are caught up in a network of formal relationships.

And speaking of a friend who has just retired from being a surgeon:

> this marks the beginning of a new career as 'doctor of the person'. Now he has time to listen to those who have never spoken freely about themselves because they are inarticulate, to those who have never received from anyone the welcome, the attention and the love that may be as vital to them as a surgical operation.[19]

If only older people could catch this vision I am sure it would transform our society. Rather than being tucked away in a lonely dark room waiting for non-existent friends to call they could be a welcome part of this friendship-hungry world, providing a listening ear and the support of a treasure chest of wisdom to all comers – and especially the young.

NB Making a New Year resolution to try to get old friends together more often and to be better about keeping in touch with people.

39

Could We Really Face Getting Another Puppy?

3rd February

Just thinking this morning that it is nearly three years since our lovely golden retriever had to be put down.

Even now there are still days when we miss her terribly – but probably not quite enough to actually want to go through the trauma of puppyhood all over again.

I can still remember all those chewed up shoes (always one of each pair and never both!); our precious lovingly tended plants disinterred from the garden (complete with as much soil as possible) and brought indoors to grace the sitting room carpet; absolutely enormous puddles and other unspeakables all over the place, and lovely smelly rubbish everywhere. Honestly don't think I could cope any more!

Besides which, now that George has retired, at least it means we are free to go away much more, and this really makes having a puppy so much more difficult.

But I always feel sad whenever I see a dog like Sasha and wish she was still with us. Though not when the rain is really bucketing down and she would still have been standing by the door wagging her tail optimistically! It's really nice now to be able to go for a walk when *we* want to and not to have to trudge out in all weathers regardless, although I am sure it did us a power of good.

When Ted and Jane were given this dear little puppy on his birthday we did seriously waver. Apparently their children had decided they needed something to keep them company after they had all left home.

At first we were all captivated – it was such an adorable fluffy little thing – but then, poor dears, they had absolutely no idea what had hit them. After nearly a month of sleepless nights, as it howled and howled below stairs, and chewed up half the house into the bargain, they eventually had to admit defeat and return the poor little creature to its original owner.

And at that point we both agreed we had made the right decision, and that we should stick to this at all costs, however much pressure people try to put on us.

So now we have this tyrannical demanding cat to deal with, who, rather like an only child, has decided she has a perfect right to every minute of our time, appearing like magic to sit on top of whatever we are doing so that we can't possibly miss seeing her or avoid paying her the attention she clearly feels she deserves.

She sits there determinedly as close to the fridge as possible, with that fierce meaningful expression on her face, and the message is clear enough: 'Feed me now or else. . . .' And of course we do – if only in desperation in order to get rid of her.

Re-reading this I think we must be getting into our dotage if animals are taking over our lives like this. It reminds me of my mother whose whole world revolved round her ancient grizzly dog in the last few years, and the desperate loss for her when she finally moved into a nursing home and had to leave him behind.

What we really need are animals pre-programmed to last as long as we do, but that's quite difficult to work out – as sadly they just never live long enough.

40

Stay Out of the Attic!

Came downstairs this morning to find George meaningfully eyeing my kitchen cupboards. I suppose they haven't been spring cleaned for quite some time. I'm sure there are plenty of interesting fossils hidden away at the very back, with sell-by dates that could even qualify them for an Antiques Food Show.

The young are always going on at us about this, and about some of the things in the fridge that are well past their sell-by dates. George is convinced that if things don't smell bad there can't be anything wrong with them (actually he has almost no sense of smell, but never mind).

Goodness, I hope this is not a sign of advancing senility! I remember cleaning out my mother-in-law's fridge when she was in her eighties and finding all kinds of hairy horrors that she was still happily consuming in blissful ignorance!

Unfortunately most of the house needs a thoroughly good turn out, but I am not really sure where to begin. I only know it will have to be a day when I actually feel like it before I can even begin to get going, and I *definitely* don't feel like it now! I suppose it will be a massive

126

relief when the job is finally over and done with.

Told George I'd make a deal with him. I would clean out the kitchen cupboards if he would do something about the room he uses for a study, from which the filing and pending trays now stretch right across the landing and onto every available surface. Judging by the muttering on the landing later I guessed that I had successfully avoided this particular issue for the time being.

Missing his secretary poor chap!

Oh dear, I suppose we really ought to be tidying up and sorting out all kinds of things so that we don't have to have some terrible purge later on, if we need to move to a smaller house, or, worse still, fall off our perches early and leave this horrific task for the young to cope with.

The trouble is that though we've travelled and lived abroad for quite a few years, we've technically owned and kept our possessions in this house for over thirty years, and the fossil evidence goes back a long way.

All of the 'children' still have things in the rooms that were theirs. And for some reason it never seems to be 'quite the right moment', or 'there isn't really room in our flat' for these to be taken. My personal theory is that they still want to keep a stake here in the family home, but anyway I don't have the heart to do anything much about this.

Then there's the attic – which is a real nightmare! You can scarcely get in the door for all of my mother's things that were just deposited there whilst we were abroad, and have been left all this time because I couldn't face going through them.

And the unending clutter goes on back from there – ancient suitcases that would probably fall apart if you put anything in them; rolls of spare wallpaper that I can scarcely remember ever having up on the wall; pictures and rugs that no longer sort of fit anywhere but one hates to finally part with, and then on back far into the cobwebby depths. Am really not sure how or when we are ever going to find the energy or enthusiasm to get this particular task over and done with.

At the very back are boxes and boxes of 'special' toys and mementos that the children deposited there for safe keeping, because they were greatly treasured at the time or being saved up for their own offspring one distant day in the future. Probably a lot of that will eventually be rejected as 'not wanted on voyage'.

The other day we unearthed a very special box belonging to Carol that she had covered with heavy black instructions 'This Box Belongs to Carol Brown. Do Not Steal or Destroy on Pain of Death'. But when it was opened now many years on, the contents were clearly highly embarrassing to her.

It was quite bitter-sweet really – lots of precious little ornaments stowed away as wonderful treasures at the time, but now seen through sophisticated adult eyes as almost totally worthless – except that they brought back memories to us of a lovely little girl delighting in quite simple things.

Maybe there's a kind of parable there about so many things that we treasure and hang onto which in later life – and especially when we've gone – turn out to be fairly worthless, except that they remind others of the people to whom they were important.

41

What Things Would We Keep to the End?

Wonderful sunrise this morning. The whole sky a sort of red gold, gradually fading as the light got stronger. It makes me wonder yet again what heaven will really be like if this is just a foretaste.

Thinking about this house and realizing that after thirty years' occupation, apart from our overseas postings, it's all the children have ever known in this country, and very much part of the family building blocks. So I suppose it really matters to them what happens here, and that they still feel very much a part of the old place.

Lying in bed in the early hours, I started wondering how on earth anyone ever manages to reduce their precious possessions down to the mere handful that they would be allowed to take with them into a tiny flat, or, worse still, a single room in an old people's home. Goodness, I don't know where I'd start.

That lovely faded miniature of my mother, the old mahogany tea caddy with inlaid highland stags, the *Daily Light* I was given so many years ago? And yet, there might be quite a freedom in this editing down.

Just remembering that when we lived in that tiny bungalow on the beach in Papua New Guinea, right under the shadow of the volcano, we were only able to take a fraction of our possessions out with us – and somehow we managed to fit this all into just two tin trunks. A few posters for the walls, some family photos to remind us of home, and just a couple of lamps and bedspreads.

Living with our bags packed and essential supplies of food and water at the ready we survived out there very happily for several years with everything we really needed close at hand. It seems quite extraordinary looking back that sometimes we even had to take our own knives and forks with us when we went out for a meal, because everyone else had only the barest essentials in their houses as well.

But life out there was so wonderfully relaxed and uncluttered, and as a result the whole experience gave us an amazing sense of freedom.

I'll never forget how difficult it was to return to England after that and to cope with all the clutter of years in our own house, but at least it taught us what was really important, and also what we could perfectly well do without!

It seems terrible when you think how people in very poor countries treasure such little scraps of things, when many of us could probably hold the jumble sale of the century.

Do not store up for yourselves treasure on earth, where moth and rust destroy and thieves break in and steal. But store up for yourselves treasures in heaven, where moth and rust do not destroy, and where thieves do not break in and steal. For where your treasure is, there your heart will be also. (Matthew 6:19–21)

42

Seeing Timothy Again

Timothy has grown so much I can hardly believe it. He's a real little person now – knows exactly what he wants as well!

So sad they live this far away, but it's lovely to be able to come up to Scotland once in a while and see them all again. This way you certainly never take each other for granted, and at least they are not thousands of miles away, as so many of our friends' grandchildren are.

A little tap on the door this morning – which fortunately he can't quite open yet – and there was Timothy bright eyed and bushy tailed, all ready to play with Gazza (not quite sure why he calls me that, but it certainly provoked some interesting comments in the shops yesterday!).

Needless to say at 6 a.m. George was not wholly enchanted with Timothy's arrival and turned over with a great hurrumphing so as to be invisible under the bed-clothes.

Oh well, at least I am well used to this time of day, though I would have quite enjoyed another half hour or so in bed. Besides which this house is absolutely freezing! Good bracing Scottish air, but George of course still has to have the windows wide open.

Anyway Timothy and I crept downstairs like a couple of conspirators, with me swathed in my duvet and a good thick pair of socks, to inspect all of his toys and have a wonderful time 'bonding' as Carol would call it.

He's a real little boy now and quite extraordinarily different after having only girls ourselves. Even before he could walk he always had this absolute obsession with wheels and trucks and anything with machinery to make it go.

Yesterday we made the big mistake of taking him to see a lovely local farm with fluffy baby animals and lots of chickens to feed. But it quickly became apparent that none of this was half as interesting as the bright yellow digger doing road repairs in the road outside.

And then to his great delight he discovered that they had push-along cars and tractors out by the stables. After that we found it virtually impossible to get him to take the slightest interest in watching the baby lambs feed or even throwing bread to the ducks on the pond. But the all-time highlight was of course a ride on a real tractor!

From George's point of view this is absolutely wonderful. At long last, after three daughters, he has someone in the family who actually *enjoys* playing with cars and trains. And there's no doubt in my mind what Timothy's next Christmas present will be: something that Grandpa will clearly enjoy every bit as much.

Just wondering about this very special bond that grandparents have with their grandchildren. It's somehow so very different from any relationship we had with our own children – a bond of real trust and understanding, rather like naughty children out doing what they think is 'fun', with no need to take personal responsibility for all the boring things you have to when you are looking after your own children.

But lovely as they are, it's wonderful to be able to hand them back when the day's play is over!

43

Space to Recover

Since this visit was never going to be exactly a 'holiday' I am really glad we allowed ourselves a few extra days to spend some time up on the west coast, and find a bit of peace and quiet after all that incredible non-stop baby chatter.

It's so absolutely beautiful at this time of year: a mass of bluebells, primroses and bright spring green leaves reflected in the mirrored surface of the lochs, with wonderful shapes of mountains half hidden in the mist.

We could be on another planet out here among the mountains. Suddenly the frantic busy outside world fades into the distance and you feel that the very heart-beat of life is all around you, with the amazing wonder of God's creation on every side.

Quite by chance we came across this lovely ruined chapel on the shores of Loch Fyne yesterday. It had obviously been a very special place for many people from all over the world, and the gravestones indicated how many of them had asked to find their last resting place here. We walked back up the hill just as the evening sunlight was adding its wonderful warm glow to the old stone walls and carefully mown grass leading down to the deep indigo waters of the loch.

Just thinking that so much of what really matters in life gets drowned out by the clutter and rush of our everyday world. We never seem to have the time to tune into what C S Lewis calls 'the deeper magic'[20].

Sometimes I get a very strong sense that much of what is rattling along on the surface of our lives keeping us so frantically busy is fairly pointless stuff. It's just that we hardly ever recognize this when we are up to our necks in it all. Like a horrible thick blanket of fog, all the chores and mundane things we have to plough through every day often smother all trace of God's lasting truth and eternity beneath their suffocating folds.

But when we come apart and take time to drink in the beauty of magnificent scenery like this and really listen in the silence for what God is trying to say to us, then suddenly all the rattle and busyness fades into the background, the fog lifts, and the whole world is transformed before our very eyes. And then we get a glimpse of that deeper magic for ourselves.

Here on the mountain I have spoken to you clearly: I will not often do so down in Narnia. Here on the mountain the air is clear and your mind is clear; as you drop down into Narnia, the air will thicken. Take great care that it does not confuse your mind. And the signs which you have learnt here will not look at all as you expect them to look, when you meet them there. That is why it is so important to know them by heart and pay no attention to appearances. Remember the signs and believe the signs. Nothing else matters.

C S Lewis[21]

44
Just Heard that Margaret Is Dying

Had the most terrible news this morning and still finding this impossible to believe.

My lovely friend Margaret is dying of leukaemia and there is absolutely nothing that they can do – it sounds from the letter as if she has only a few more weeks or even days to live. Just can't imagine life without her around.

Everyone is praying for healing of course, but there was something about her letter that sounded so very final: 'I still spend most of the day on my bed, and I find the most mundane physical exercise like walking upstairs totally exhausting ... they say that the leukaemia cells have now invaded my liver ... my only aim now is to stay at home as long as possible.'

Apparently it's too late now for any kind of treatment, and it sounds as if that's a real relief to her – and of course it's true that so often this only seems to prolong the agony.

Thank God that her faith is so alive and real to her. Fred told me tonight that through all her suffering she is just so very aware of the presence of Jesus there with her holding her. He sounds absolutely desperate, poor love.

Do so wish we lived nearer to be some real support to them both.

North Yorkshire seems such a terribly long way, and I'm really not sure whether in the present situation it would be more or less of a burden to have someone else in the house. I think from what he said they are just clinging onto what precious few days they have left together.

Goodness, I can hardly bear thinking about it, and everything in me just longs to be able to do something to help.

Just praying that God will give them both the strength to cope and that he will make these last few precious moments of time they have together endurable and somehow very special.

Even though I walk
through the valley of the shadow of death,
I will fear no evil,
for you are with me;
your rod and your staff
they comfort me. (Psalm 23:4)

45
My Father's Birthday

30th July

My father's birthday today – it suddenly hit me as I was reading the paper and glanced up at the date.

We used to always have such a wonderful time on this day when he was still alive. A special lunch for him at The Swan near their house, and then some exciting visit to the theatre or a film in the evening.

Strange, but it seems quite wrong just to be going on with life as if nothing of any importance happened on this day of all days.

He was such a lovely warm man with an enormous smile that my mother used to describe as 'a ripe melon splitting', and I really miss him still.

Strange that I should find myself thinking of this today when he died so many years ago, but I suppose there's still a big father-shaped hole in my life somewhere.

Now that my mother is dead too, and in fact all of our children's four grandparents, it feels very lonely and exposed sometimes to be top of the heap with no one older to turn to.

In fact it seems *totally incredible* to realize that we are the grandparents now and the buck stops here.

Whatever may happen to you, God is your father, and he is always interested in you, and that is his attitude towards you.

Martyn Lloyd-Jones[22]

46

Not Seeing Enough of My Girlfriends

15th August

Just realized this morning that now George is at home so much of the time, I seldom get round to seeing my other friends.

I always wondered why I lost touch with Jane so easily after Peter retired, but now I am beginning to realize what it is like. It's so easy just to settle down as a comfortable twosome and forget about the rest of the world, and you really do have to make a conscious effort to keep in touch.

Of course it's lovely having George here – at least most of the time – and when he is not busy telling me how to run everything. But really I do miss having a good natter with my 'girlfriends' and a chance to catch up with what is going on in the world.

'You can always talk to me,' he says endearingly, making it obvious he doesn't have the least idea what this kind of 'talking' is about.

And whenever I've been on the phone to a girlfriend, he usually makes some rather pointed comment such as 'I can't imagine what you find to talk about for all that time . . . no wonder our phone bill is so high.'

Yesterday I didn't get to the phone in time, and found

to my embarrassment that the answerphone had faith-
fully recorded my every word – and worse still that
George was just sitting there afterwards listening to it in
absolute amazement.

'Well, you really do both rabbit on, don't you? I could
have said that in half the time.'

He was definitely out of favour for quite a while after
that comment!

Still no doubt it will give him something to talk about
in the men's group when it meets tomorrow. I'd certainly like to be a fly on the wall there. But it's really good
that they've got this bolt hole, and I'm sure they're
much happier without us around to disagree.

47

Fred Dropping In All Margaret's Clothes

5th September

Fred dropped in this morning on his way into London to see the solicitor and finally settle the probate on Margaret's will. He was looking so haggard and drawn that it almost hurt me to look at him, and I just wanted to gather him up in my arms and somehow take the terrible pain away.

Did my best to make him feel comfortable and unwind a bit. I sat him down in his favourite armchair and played some of the music I know he likes – but he seemed totally on edge like a very taut string, and unable to really settle anywhere. I guess he's afraid that if he allows himself to really relax then the pain and the memories will come flooding back, but if only he could just let go and cry.

Poor love – I think he'd been clearing out all Margaret's things and finally facing up to the fact that she has really gone and he is on his own now. It must be so dreadful for him.

Wish we lived nearer so that we could be there for him. It's so sad that their children are right over the other side of the world. At least they did manage to fly back for the funeral, but it seems to me that this is just the time he needs them most. I suppose they had to get back to Australia and to their respective jobs, but I really wish they could have stayed that little bit longer.

That's one of the problems with the world today – so many of our families now seem to be scattered across the planet, and seldom really close enough to help each other when the going gets tough.

Fred left me this enormous bag full of Margaret's clothes that he thought I might like. It's so kind of him, but if the truth be told I can hardly bear to look through them. They probably won't fit me anyway, but then neither can I bear to take them down to the charity shop.

That lovely pale yellow sweater that looked so good on her, the fantastically elegant dress that she got in the summer sales two years ago, and the battered old jacket she so often wore in the garden. It seems really strange that she has gone on without all these familiar things that were so very much a part of her.

Of course I know perfectly well that she won't need them where she has gone now, but it's impossible somehow to imagine her without them – though I know that sounds really stupid.

I guess it's not unlike a wonderful technicolour butterfly that has discarded its chrysalis and been transformed into a completely new creation, freed at last to leave the earth and rise on the currents of the summer air at will, and no longer condemned just to plod hopelessly around on the earth. But goodness how I wish I could see the butterfly!

I know she will be much happier now and released from all that terrible pain she endured in those last few weeks. Am trying hard to think of her now and imagining her standing in the courts of heaven, full of wonder at everything before her and finally free from all the burdens that have worn her down over the last few months.

I am really touched that she has left me her Bible. It's so well worn that some of the leaves are almost transparent, and the best loved chapters are close to falling apart. But I reckon that's pretty clear evidence of how much this precious little book meant to her. Almost every page has special passages marked out, and verses underlined that had obviously really spoken to her. And I have always loved that special prayer of St Francis of Assisi that she kept on the fly leaf.

Lord make me an instrument of your peace,
Where there is hatred let me bring your love,
Where there is injury pardon,
Where there is doubt, faith,
Where there is despair, hope,
Where there is darkness light,
Where there is sadness, joy.

Grant that I may not so much seek
To be consoled as to console,
To be understood as to understand,
To be loved as to love.
For it is in giving that we receive,
It is in pardoning that we are pardoned,
And it is in dying
That we are born to eternal life.

I will never forget that Margaret was the first person to really bring my faith alive for me, and I owe her so much. She lived out her whole life in loving others around her, and you simply couldn't help but catch that love for yourself.

There was never any doubt about the fact that Jesus

was so very real to her. Fred said that just before she died she kept asking him, 'Can't you see Jesus? He was here in the room just now. . . . I think he is waiting for me to go home with him.'

I have absolutely no doubt that she is safe and at peace with him now, but goodness how I am going to miss her.

The Last Enemy

And he who each day
reveals a new masterpiece of sky
and whose joy
can be seen in the eyelash of a child
who when he hears our smug indifference
can whisper an ocean into lashing fury
and talk tigers into padding roars.
This is my God
whose breath is in the wings of eagles
whose power is etched in crags of mountains.
It is he whom I will meet.
And in whose presence I will find tulips and clouds
kneeling martyrs and trees
the whole vast praising of his endless creation
and he will grant the uniqueness
that eluded me
in my earthly bartering with Satan.
That day when he will erase the painful gasping of
      my ego
and I will sink my face into the wonder of his glorylove
and I will watch as planets converse with sparrows.
On that day
when death is finally dead.

                                                Stewart Henderson[23]

48

Wondering What Margaret Is Doing Now

Thinking about Margaret again in the early hours and wondering what she is doing now.

I love that image of a ship leaving behind the shores of this life and disappearing over the horizon, and as it finally vanishes from our sight, drawing near to the shores of that other world that God has promised to all those who love him.

Just thinking too about all our own loved ones waiting to welcome us on the other side, and how wonderful it will be to see them again. It's an extraordinary thought and one that I've scarcely stopped to consider before.

I really hope I will find them all there, and that some of them reached out to God in the last few precious moments of their lives, because certainly one or two of them really didn't want to know about him before that.

How lovely to think of meeting my parents again and my little brother whom I haven't seen since he died when I was seven years old. I wonder what we will think of each other now so many years later? Or will we just be bowled over by the wonder of life in heaven and overjoyed to see each other again?

'He will wipe every tear from their eyes. There will be no more death or mourning or crying or pain, for the old order of things has passed away' (Revelation 21:4).

Just thinking how strange it is that we hardly ever hear anyone talk much about heaven these days – except perhaps in those incredible Hollywood pseudo 'supernatural' films. But I wonder why that is?

We seem so fully preoccupied with keeping our physical bodies functioning properly, and remembering to take enough exercise and plenty of vitamins. And then we are so busy improving on every kind of skill from photography to upholstery and all stations in between – and of course that's all great! But why does nobody ever talk about time and eternity and the fact that not one single one of us will be around on this planet for ever?

I remember watching the video of some old black and white film that someone gave George on his sixtieth, all about what happened in the year that he was born. There were lots of wobbling figures staggering across the screen with that strange fast moving gait that many of the early films suffered from.

And we were just watching some very scratchy faded old footage taken on Ascot Racecourse some sixty years previously, when suddenly a friend who was staying with us came out with the kind of remark guaranteed to stop everyone short in their tracks: 'Isn't it strange to think that every single one of those people is dead now?'

George and I have never forgotten that moment of realization, and actually it had quite a salutary effect on both of us.

We are living the only life that we will ever have, and yet it is so unbelievably easy to squander the time and fill the days up with just any old thing.

Apparently when Billy Graham was once asked the question 'What surprises you most about life?', he replied quite simply 'Its brevity.'

Crossing the Bar

Sunset and evening star,
And one clear call for me!
And may there be no moaning of the bar,
When I put out to sea.

But such a tide as moving seems asleep,
Too full for sound and foam,
With that which drew from out the boundless deep
Turns home again.

Twilight and evening bell
And after that the dark!
And may there be no sadness of farewell
When I embark;

For tho' from out our bourne of Time and Place
The flood may bear me far,
I hope to see my Pilot face to face
When I have crost the bar.

Alfred, Lord Tennyson

49

Extraordinary Ideas Some People Have about Life After Death!

14th September

Watching that very weird programme on TV last night, it's hard to believe just how far away from the truth some people's ideas about heaven and eternity are today.

I can hardly believe this extraordinary obsession with freezing or preserving people's bodies (or, as a cheap economy alternative, just their heads!) so that they will be ready for another incarnation. You would think that all these thousands of years after the Egyptians mummified their kings and buried treasure for them to use in the afterlife we might have made some progress – but apparently not!

It never fails to amaze me that some people seem happy to put their whole faith and trust in flimsy man-made theories like this, when the whole question of their eternal life hangs in the balance.

Reading Max Sinclair's book *Living in the Light of Heaven* he comments that so many people pray for a swift unconscious death, but that actually 'if we don't face death for ourselves then we don't ever get to thinking about heaven'[24]. Or in other words heaven only comes into the picture if we honestly and thoughtfully face our mortality.

Apparently an old Church of England prayer asks

that we should be 'delivered from sudden death' in order that we can make our peace with God and prepare for where we are going.

Margaret wrote to me with these words shortly before she died: 'A cousin of ours was killed by a motorcyclist last week. It makes me realize how lucky I am to have forewarning of my death so that I can mend some fences with God.'

I suppose that we are all so terribly caught up with this present life and focused on some very earthly concerns around us, that it matters more than ever that we are given notice of the fact that we will actually all be dying in the not so very distant future.

One of the things that has always struck me about people who have just survived some terrible trauma or tragedy is that they return to their everyday lives with a whole new perspective, and a determination to make each day count for something, and to really love others around them. They have finally realized that the life they so nearly lost is really precious and never to be wasted again.

My command is this: Love each other as I have loved you. Greater love has no-one than this, that he lay down his life for his friends. You are my friends if you do what I command. I no longer call you servants, because a servant does not know his master's business. Instead, I have called you friends, for everything that I learned from my Father I have made known to you. You did not choose me, but I chose you and appointed you to go and bear fruit – fruit that will last. Then the Father will give you whatever you ask in my name. This is my command: Love each other. (John 15:12–17)

50

A Second Chance at Life?

Trying to imagine how it would feel to be dramatically rescued at the eleventh hour from some tragic death and miraculously given a second chance to live.

Can only get a very faint image of how it might seem, but I am sure that the whole of life would suddenly seem really precious and sparkling, clear as a bright new spring morning. Who knows, I might even be grateful for all those really boring mundane things like housework and ironing that I grumble my way through at present! And lots of other pointless rubbishy things that clutter up my precious time at the moment would surely be jettisoned overboard at the earliest possible opportunity.

Had I really been on the verge of death, then all of those things I had so longed to do before leaving this life would be very deeply engraved on my conscious mind, so that now of course there would be no stopping me. In fact I would probably go into overdrive!

It suddenly brings into sharp relief how the world might be when I am no longer around – and what I would want to leave to our children and grandchildren who come after us. Not just 'things' and 'material security' but a truly deep sense of being truly loved and cared about.

Desperately as I love them now, there is nothing I can do to protect them from harm or to help them in the future, when the going gets tough and we are no longer here. But I *can* still pray for them, and ask the One who loves them far more than I ever can, to keep them safe from harm.

Decided to make a list of all the things I want to achieve in however many years God gives me, thus making sure I can't leave out things that I would much rather forget.

- Write all those letters I have been meaning to write for months to people I really care about but never see because they are too far away.
- Write special letters to my children that will hopefully make a difference to their lives in many years to come – above all telling them how much I love them.
- Arrange to meet up with friends we never get round to seeing (and only write to at Christmas time) because we are just too busy and have allowed our diaries to become too full. Arrange get-togethers, meet people too far away for lunches or picnics half-way there.
- Try to see as much of our friends as possible – spend valuable time with them, listening and sharing.
- Make more time to 'be' in the silence listening to God. Find a place that is special where I can do this – perhaps with a lovely view out into the garden, and where I am not surrounded by everyday clutter.
- Make more effort to read my Bible and to really study something in greater depth – amazingly good

when I get round to this, but it hardly ever happens.

- Remember to pray for the children and grand-children – that God will take care of them now and in the distant future when we are no longer around for them.
- Remember to visit people in hospital or housebound who are out of the swing of life.
- Try to remember friends' birthdays and anniversaries that I so often forget – hopeless!
- Think about learning some completely new subject to give me a fresh kick-start and interest.
- Brush up on my languages – resuscitate what is down there, take it out and dust it for use!
- Keep on painting – and never let the busyness crowd this out.
- Spend at least half an hour a day reading something worthwhile – and not just collapsed exhausted in front of the television!
- Take a fresh look at the garden and see what I can improve and grow to get more in touch with God's creation, and make something really beautiful there.
- Get rid of all the rubbish in the attic and find good homes for anything that might be of any use.
- Make more time to really talk and listen to one another instead of just filling the time with any old thing.
- Ask God if there is something new and special he wants me to do in this final chapter of my life – and make me ready to listen.

Above all, I want to set sail on this final voyage home with God as my pilot, launching out into the deep uncharted waters of his river of life and trusting him to carry me safely onwards for as long as it takes.

Swarms of living creatures will live wherever the river flows. There will be large numbers of fish, because this water flows there and makes the salt water fresh; so where the river flows everything will live.... Fruit trees of all kinds will grow on both banks of the river. Their leaves will not wither, nor will their fruit fail. Every month they will bear, because the water from the sanctuary flows to them. Their fruit will serve for food and their leaves for healing. (Ezekiel 47:9, 12)

Notes

[1] Inscription from the clock on Chester Cathedral.

[2] C S Lewis, 'The Weight of Glory', in *Screwtape Proposes a Toast* (Fontana, 1965).

[3] Anonymous, attributed to a seventeenth-century nun.

[4] John Eddison, *The Last Lap* (Kingsway Publications, 1986), p. 17.

[5] From 'Ode: Intimations of Immortality from Recollections of Early Childhood'.

[6] Enid Shelmerdine, *The Times*, April 1999.

[7] John Eddison, *The Last Lap*, p. 106.

[8] Quoted by Rob Parsons, *The Sixty Minute Father* (Hodder).

[9] Siegfried Sassoon, from *Collected Poems 1908–56* (Faber and Faber).

[10] Jenny Joseph, from *Selected Poems* (Bloodaxe, 1992).

[11] Paul Tournier, *Learning to Grow Old* (Highland, 1985), p. 32.

[12] Elaine Storkey, *The Search for Intimacy* (Hodder, 1995), p. 70.

[13] C G Jung, *Psychology of the Spirit* (Guild of Pastoral Psychology, 1933).

[14] Henri Nouwen, *The Road to Daybreak* (DLT, 1997), p. 113.

[15] John Eddison, *The Last Lap*, p. 67.

[16] George Congreve, in *The Lion Christian Quotation Collection*.

[17] C S Lewis, 'The Weight of Glory', in *Screwtape Proposes a Toast* (Fontana, 1965).

[18] In *Collected Poems* (Jonathan Cape, 1939).

[19] Paul Tournier, *Learning to Grow Old*, p. 45.

[20] C S Lewis in *The Lion, the Witch and the Wardrobe* (Geoffrey Bles, 1950).

[21] C S Lewis, *The Silver Chair* (Geoffrey Bles, 1953).

[22] In *Lion Christian Quotations*.

[23] 'The Last Enemy' in *Assembled in Britain* (Marshall Pickering, 1986), reprinted by permission of the author.

[24] Max Sinclair, *Living in the Light of Heaven* (Hodder, 1997), p. 52.